EX LIBRIS
Dana Q. Coffield

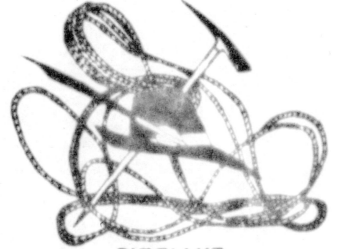

Rondoy

RONDOY

An Expedition to the Peruvian Andes

DAVID WALL

WITH A FOREWORD BY
Don Whillans

JOHN MURRAY

Printed in Great Britain by
Butler & Tanner Ltd, Frome
and London

Dedicated to the Memory of
Peter Bebbington and Graham Sadler
who died while returning from
the summit of Rondoy
on Wednesday, 7 August 1963

Foreword by Don Whillans

Rondoy is an ice peak in the Peruvian Andes and little was known about it to the small group of students from the London School of Economics, except that the formidable Italian climber, Walter Bonatti, had retreated from the final ridge. Further words as to its difficulty would seem superfluous.

Undeterred, they overcame every obstacle from raising finance to unearthing donkeys in the isolated villages of the High Andes, and still maintained a close friendship combined with a sense of humour so essential when hardship has to be endured for long periods. After several setbacks and in the face of approaching bad weather they reached the highest point on Rondoy, but only after difficult and dangerous climbing along the final ridge. But at the moment of victory, as so often happens in the beautiful surroundings of mountains, death struck, swiftly, silently and without warning, carrying two of the summit party to their deaths.

The spirit in which the whole of the expedition was carried out should be an inspiration to all adventure-loving young people, who can achieve what they desire if they try. The price of Rondoy was high, but it is people of their spirit that provide the power for progress in the world.

KATHMANDU
September 1964

Contents

Illustrations

Illustrations

The photographs were taken by Vic Walsh except when indicated as follows: [1] by the author; [2] by Charles Powell; [3] by Dave Condict; [4] by Pete Farrell

Maps

Rondoy

General map of Peru showing Rondoy

Introduction

Rondoy is a mountain of 19,300 feet. It lies at the northern end of the Cordillera Huayhuash, a range of mountains in Central Peru. An expedition from the London School of Economics Mountaineering Club had visited the area in 1961, when its leader, Peter Bebbington, had been impressed by the challenge that Rondoy offered. He later described Rondoy as: '. . . nearly 20,000 feet high, and never climbed by man. Several groups', he went on, 'have tried to climb it but it has turned them all back. Even the legendary Italian climber, Walter Bonatti, whose exploits on climbs of extreme difficulty in the Alps and Himalayas have brought him the reputation of being one of the world's greatest living climbers, had to retreat from Rondoy after two days and nights forcing a way painfully up the north face, without food, water or shelter. The reputation of Rondoy has grown as it defeated the attempts to climb it, until it is now regarded with awe by the Peruvians, and as one of the last great challenges to be overcome by men.

'In form, it is a three-sided pyramid of rock and ice, rearing up from the glaciers which skirt its base, high into the regions where the air is thin and every movement costs tremendous effort of will and muscle. Normally the easiest way up a mountain lies up its ridges, but on Rondoy the ridges are dangerous. Steep and narrow, knife-edged in parts, they are capped by wind-blown ice formations. In places these are fragile and brittle, so that a clumsy move on the part of the climber would send him rattling down the sheer ice-walls below: in places soft and sagging, like the snow that hangs from the roofs of houses in a thaw, ready to fall silently away, hundreds of tons at a time, with no warning to the climber who may be making his way over them. The only chance to find a way to the top of Rondoy is to try the faces. These appear impossibly steep for normal climbing, with craggy rock outcrops jutting out of the blue ice, overhung by the cornices on the ridge, and periodically swept by avalanches and rock-falls, through which the climber must pick a route. The only way to get up a face like this is to work a way up one of the ribs or bulges that seam the face, clear of the avalanches.'

Excited by this description, David Condict and myself, both at the time members of the London School of Economics Mountaineering Club, asked Pete if he would be prepared to lead another expedition to Peru. Before going to L.S.E., Pete had spent two years in the Navy and had loved it. He had always loved to be out and about, and while still at school had been awarded the Queen Scout's badge. He disliked a settled, sedentary way of life, especially in London. In fact he had returned from Peru only with the object of doing research on Latin America, and with the fixed intention of going back to Peru at the first opportunity. When we approached him, he had already made his plans to return to Lima with his wife, and was therefore only too pleased to have this chance of making an attempt on Rondoy.

Condict and I had had little experience of snow and ice climbing; in fact that summer, 1962, saw us on our first Alpine meet. It was essential to find more experienced climbers to join us if we were to make a serious attempt. In Chamonix we met Charles Powell, an L.S.E. graduate with several Alpine seasons to his credit. At that time he was working as an instructor for the Mountaineering Association, but he readily agreed to join our expedition. At the same time we met Graham Sadler, a contemporary of Bebbington and Powell. Since he graduated, he had been teaching economics at the Matthew Boulton College in Birmingham. Graham had had four Alpine seasons and was a welcome addition to the team. He offered to help us with the organization as much as he could from Birmingham.

Pete Bebbington had stayed on in Lima for several months after the 1961 expedition, working for an English-language newspaper.

During those months he had met the advance party of an expedition from New Zealand, consisting of Vic Walsh and Pete Farrell, who had both emigrated from the United Kingdom some years earlier. Pete Bebbington now suggested that we should invite them to join us, as both had had considerable experience not only in the New Zealand Alps but also in the Peruvian Andes. We were all able to meet Vic in London in November 1962, as he had come over to work in Fleet Street after the New Zealand Alpine Club's expedition. He agreed at once to come with us.

Between our return to London from the Alps in September 1962, and the Christmas vacation, the six of us had got the expedition off the ground. Sir Alexander Carr-Saunders and Professor T. Graham-Brown agreed to act as sponsors, and—most important of all—the Everest Foundation had promised us financial backing. After the vacation we felt confident of the expedition reaching Peru, and wrote to Pete Farrell in New Zealand, inviting him also to join us. To assist with his passage from New Zealand to Peru, we submitted a supplementary request to the Everest Foundation. We had a favourable reply from both within a month, by which time the expedition had another member, Peter Westnidge, who was a member of the L.S.E. club in his finals year, and a more than competent rock climber. With Pete Farrell and Vic Walsh included in the party we felt justified in adding the peaks of Jirishanca and Yerupaja to our programme. In the event, we were to climb neither.

When Pete Farrell and Pete Westnidge had both agreed to join us the expedition took its final form. Six of us were either at, or had graduated at, the London School of Economics, and all of those six except Pete Westnidge and I had started their climbing career with the School's Mountaineering Club. Graham, Dave Condict, Pete Westnidge and I had all gone up to University straight from the sixth-form and were younger than the other four; Graham was twenty-four, Dave Condict was twenty-one, Pete Westnidge was twenty, and I was twenty-two. The other four had all served in the Armed Forces: Charlie and Pete Bebbington before going up to L.S.E.: Pete Farrell and Vic before emigrating to New Zealand. Charlie was twenty-eight, Pete Bebbington twenty-five, Pete Farrell twenty-four, and Vic twenty-seven.

January saw us getting down to the details of organization. Vic Walsh and Pete Westnidge looked after the equipment. Even this drudgery had its lighter side, as when one of Pete's begging letters brought us the offer from an Oxford Street shop of trade prices on skirts and blouses. Charlie co-ordinated the appeals to food manufacturers, who on the whole supported us well, and to whom we are very grateful. Without their help this expedition and many others would not have taken place.

Pete Bebbington, as leader, dealt with such climbing authorities as the Everest Foundation; and also with the Peruvian officials, who allocated the north-west face of Rondoy to us and the more difficult south-east face to Lief Patterson's American expedition. He also acted as co-ordinating officer. Graham helped wherever he could in writing the necessary letters. My job was that of secretary and treasurer, which included liaison with the college. I also held the unenviable position of Keeper of the Expedition Telephone. To Dave Condict fell the arrangement of transport—a complicated task, because the seven of us travelling from England were obliged, owing to the dates of our examinations, to go in three separate groups. Pete Bebbington would be the last to leave, as he was sitting for a teacher's certificate at the training college at Avery Hill. Dave Condict and Pete Westnidge, who were taking finals at L.S.E. in June, would travel with Graham, Charlie, and Vic. Graham was on the other side of the examination hurdle, having to set and mark papers in the Matthew Boulton College. Charlie also was examining, at Catford College of Commerce. Pete Farrell, in New Zealand, was making his own travel arrangements. I myself, being the only one who could leave earlier, was to sail on June 1st in the *Reina del Mar* with the equipment, and to arrange for its release as soon as possible from the Peruvian Customs. The plan was that, by the time the main party arrived, I should be in Chiquian (from where we were to trek into the mountains) with all the forty-six crates of equipment. It was not to turn out quite like that.

Vic, Graham, Charlie, Pete Westnidge, and Dave Condict were to travel together at the end of June. They were to fly to New York on a charter flight, drive by hired car to Miami and then take a night plane to Lima. Pete Bebbington was to take the same route, except that he would travel by Greyhound bus instead of hired car; he was to travel out early in July. Pete Farrell would have to leave home first: travelling by sea from New Zealand to Panama and then flying down, he was expected in Lima at the end of June.

While we were making our preparations in London, we heard from our Vice-President, Don Whillans. He told us that, while he was in Patagonia on the Towers of Peigne expedition, he had met Ferrari, a member of the Italian expedition which had attempted Rondoy in 1961. Ferrari had sent us a message via Don, short and to the point. It said: 'Watch your steps on Rondoy.'

The only available photograph of that face of Rondoy that we were to attempt, was made by this Italian expedition. It was a poor photograph, so poor in fact that it wasn't until we had actually climbed Rondoy that we realized from which direction it was taken. We learned enough from it, however, to appreciate that it was basically going to be a problem in snow and ice. The only other photographs of Rondoy that we had were two in Schneider's book, taken from the opposite side from that on which our attempt was to be made; and one in John Sack's account of the Harvard expedition's ascent of Yerupaja, which bore the caption: 'The avalanche-scoured face of Rondoy.'

In May we packed the food and equipment that had accumulated over the preceding months in the club locker. It took over forty-two crates altogether. We started work on a Saturday morning, suffering from hangovers, after a party the night before at

Introduction

which all the England-based members had met for the first time as one group. We worked throughout the day in a courtyard stacked high with toilet rolls, tins of syrup, and ice-axes.

Even though we did not stop for lunch, we were still surprised by the early arrival of the B.R.S. lorry that was to take the crates to the Liverpool docks. At last we nailed down the last lid, on which Pete Westnidge deftly painted its number and expedition mark. The lorry eventually drove off, leaving behind four crates which would have to travel with me as accompanied baggage.

I left for Liverpool a week later; it was to be a month before I saw any of the others again. The *Reina del Mar* sailed from Liverpool on June 1st carrying an advance party of one, together with the food and equipment of the London School of Economics Andean Expedition, 1963.

ACKNOWLEDGEMENTS

Our first thanks—those for making the expedition possible—go to the Everest Foundation for a generous grant; to the Friends of the London School of Economics for a gift of equipment; to the many manufacturers who gave us food and equipment or allowed us trade prices; and to the Pacific Steam Navigation Company for carrying our crates to Peru free of charge.

Next, our thanks to those who helped us on our way: to the staff (especially the porters) of the London School of Economics for assistance in all forms; to Mr & Mrs Kanemerian of New York, and Mr & Mrs Hendricks of Florida, for accommodation while travelling through the U.S.A.; to Gustavo Lama and David Lewis in Lima for accommodation in Lima and also for much valuable assistance in many other forms; to the *Club Andino Peruano* and especially its President, Señor Caesar Morales Arnao and

Acknowledgements

his sisters for their help in the arduous task of getting the expedition out of Lima and on its way to the mountains; to Colin Darbyshire, an ex-patriate member of the Climbers' Club living in Lima, a fact which eventually gains the gratitude of every Andean expedition passing through that capital; to Eduardo (Ted) Ramirez of Chiquian for help in getting the expedition onto its feet in Chiquian and also for his assistance after the accident.

We would also like to record a deep debt of thanks to those who helped us after the accident, in addition to those who have already been mentioned. They are: Derek Fabian, for advice and material assistance; the staff of the British Embassy, Lima; the New York office of B.O.A.C.; and the British Universities' North America Club.

I would like to add my personal thanks to those who helped me write this book, namely: John G. Murray, Mrs K. West, and Graham Watson (of Curtis-Brown Ltd) who gave me much advice, encouragement, and assistance—they are in fact largely responsible for the final appearance of the book; to Robert Sadler for the loan of a photostatic copy of his brother's diary, and to David Condict and Peter Westnidge for the loan of their diaries; to David Garrett for reading the manuscript and making a number of useful suggestions; and last, but far from least, my wife, Nancy, for her help, patience, and tolerance during the time I was writing the book and preparing it for the printer. She also read and corrected the manuscript and proofs, and is largely responsible for the index.

London, August 1964

1

Lima: A City of Contrasts

It is difficult to describe Lima except through its most obvious attribute: the contrasts between wealth and poverty, the old and the new. Capital of the land of the Incas, it holds a place in the imagination of the Westerner as a city of mystique, of exotic ways of life, and of erotic pleasures: a romantic city. Western writers needing some symbol of strangeness will use Lima as a metaphor complete in itself.

Yet my first impression of Lima was one of ordinariness. Ordinary in the sense of showing characteristic features of all big cities: dock-side cafés, industrial estates, phoenix-like housing estates rising straight out of the desert, huge modern office blocks, and mad, mad, rush hours. The city man like myself feels quite at home there.

On the day the *Reina del Mar* arrived at Callao harbour, the outport for Lima, disembarking passengers had to present themselves for Immigration Control. We were told that the officials would be on board the boat at 4 a.m. Growling with surprise at the cold, sixty or so passengers straggled into the lounge at the prescribed time. And here we learned our first lesson about Peru: that two separate times co-exist in Lima. There is *Hora Peruana* (Peruvian time) and there is *Hora Inglese* (English time). Unless otherwise stated, the operative time is the local one. For whereas *Hora Inglese* means that punctuality is required, *Hora Peruana* implies that an error margin of several hours should be allowed for. On this occasion, we discovered that Peruvian time was in operation, and it was seven o'clock before passports were being checked. The three hours were not, however, wasted, for we could watch the dawn light paint an impressive study in grey. Bobbing lights across the harbour became a fleet of warships at anchor. The harbour buildings themselves looked close. The traditional greys of warships and harbours were emphasized by the overcast sky and the dull sea. Even the sea birds, monstrous pelicans, were grey. It comes as a surprise to discover that much of Peru's economic stability over many decades has been connected with these birds. In recent years their food—anchovies—has been stolen from them and processed into fishmeal, which at present accounts for some 20% of Peru's earnings of foreign exchange; while in the past, the economic development of Peru—what little there was—was largely financed by the export of bird-droppings. In 1862 this commodity, called *guano*, accounted for 65% of the foreign exchange earnings of Peru.

Callao is a depressing harbour at the best of times. Early on a winter morning it is especially so. It was therefore cheering, as we were slowly edging our way past the anchored warships, to hear the call for breakfast. After breakfast, during the course of which the ship had docked, I went on deck, hoping to locate our agent on the quay. But he never appeared, having been misinformed as to the date of my arrival. His absence only increased my misgivings about negotiating four crates of food and equipment, as parts of my personal luggage, through the legendary Peruvian Customs. My fears were more than borne out. The Peruvian Customs are like a game; I lost heavily.

My suspicions were first aroused by a little man at the foot of the gangplank who trapped me and explained that I was not allowed to take my own baggage through, but must, he said, hire him to do it for me. As soon as he found out that I was a member of a climbing expedition, he produced from the inner reaches of his pockets a collection of testimonials from leaders of previous expeditions, testifying to his adeptness in negotiating the terrors of the official sheds. This had obviously been many years ago.

Rondoy

Beginning to feel my lack of Spanish, I submissively surrendered to him the documents for the baggage. As the four crates travelling with me as accompanied personal baggage were large, unwieldy, and covered with nails and wire, the porters left them on the quay until everyone else's baggage had been taken to the customs shed. This prevented damage to suitcases and trunks, but meant a long wait before I could even hope to be cleared. When they at last arrived in the customs shed the crates were stacked behind all the luggage already there, no mean feat. Rush hour at Oxford Circus Underground station bears no comparison to the Callao Customs after a ship has been berthed. As soon as I entered the shed I retired to a large crate of machinery where I sat smoking and watching the antics of the two opposing groups: the passengers and the officials. With four large wooden crates to manœuvre, my position was hopeless. And anyway my porter had disappeared with the documents, so that there was not much else that I could do. After four hours had passed, and almost all the other passengers had left, I began to feel a little impatient. The porter returned to tell me that he was going off to lunch and would be back in three hours! One of the most frustrating features of Lima is the three-hour lunch break, during which it is impossible to do anything more than eat, drink, or sleep: which is fine, except when there is something you need doing. I went off to have lunch with a friend who lived near by.

Three hours later the clerk, who had actually begun to examine the markings on the crates, discovered that they were part of a larger consignment, the rest of which had travelled as cargo in the *Reina*. He couldn't pass them until he had the bill-of-lading, which was in our agent's hands. And of course our agent wasn't there. I rang him up and appealed to him to come and rescue me. He was too busy, he said, but I should ring him the next morning. The game was losing its entertainment value.

I gave up for the day and went off to find the hotel Pete Bebbington had suggested. The taxi took me to Lima, and drove twice up and down the street indicated on the map that Pete had drawn; but no 'Hotel los Andes' appeared. The driver, who had never heard of it, said he knew the hotel where most of the expeditions stayed. We drove there and I booked in.

The road from the docks to Lima provides an interesting introduction to Peru. In the course of four miles, most aspects of Peruvian life are encountered. In Callao itself are the very well-paid workers in the booming fish and fish-product industry. Wages are phenomenal; a man can earn more in a week than his father earned in his whole lifetime. I was told that the skipper of a little fishing smack can earn up to £150 in a week at the height of the fishing season. Never having been encouraged to save, these men scarcely know how to spend the money they are earning. Largely illiterate, their usual solution is to take several 'wives' and have children by all of them, thus helping to make the Peruvian birth rate—at approximately fifty live births per 1,000 population per annum—one of the highest in the world. (The birth rate of Brazil, by comparison, is 26 per thou. p/a.) The other main outlets for their money are drinking and gambling. In consequence, Callao abounds with children and drunkards, and with dockside bars filled with men playing dice.

The second feature of the Callao area that struck me was the arrangement of transport facilities by class/income groups. At the bottom of the scale are the trams, enormous grey monsters racing along at breakneck speed, literally overflowing, with people hanging on in every imaginable place, and uniformed schoolboys balancing on the buffers. As with all public transport in Lima, they have only one basic fare, regardless of distance travelled; and this varies only with route, age of passenger, and time of day. Tram users are in the main Indians, poor half-breeds, and school-children. Next in the rising social scale come the buses, painted like the trams in the regulation Lima grey. They are usually very long Mercedes with their engines growling constantly and impatiently at the rear. Their users seemed in the main to be the lower orders of the white-collared group—shop assistants, young clerical workers, and college students. The buses are much cleaner than the trams. They have upholstered seats, and no hangers-on outside.

Our own most popular form of transport while we were in town was the *collectivo* system. A *collectivo* is an ordinary motorcar which runs along a fixed route, from somewhere near the centre of the city to a point way out in the suburbs. Again there is only one tariff, and, as the *collectivos* are privately owned, no allowance is made for age or time of day; except that after midnight there is a 50% surcharge. The charge does vary, however, with the route, being most expensive on the least used routes and cheapest on the most popular. Not only does the fare vary between routes, but also with the type of car. The cars range from original T-model Fords with no windows, no mudguards, no bonnet, and filled to the brim with people, which run on the routes from the *barriada* slums, up to the latest American models with passengers limited to a maximum of five, on the Lima–Callao route. On the route I used most, between Lima and the suburb Miraflores, the cars were mainly last year's American model, with the occasional English or French one. The fixed charge was 2 *soles* (6½*d.*) whether you travelled one block or the whole five miles.

The *collectivo* system can only work because of the lay-out of the Lima roads. Streets in the centre are all at right-angles, cutting down-town Lima into a system of squares (*cuadras*). Radiating from the periphery of this central area are wide, straight, dual carriageways to all the suburbs. This plan allows traffic to filter into a slow lane and a fast lane, enabling the *collectivos* to pick up and drop passengers anywhere along their routes. The *collectivos* are an important and efficient part of the Lima transport system. It is a pity that such a system would not work in London.

After the *collectivos* come the taxis and limousines, the main difference between them, apart from the types of cars, being that the taxis still have fixed charges within the city limits, whereas the limousines are free to charge whatever they think they can get.

Just outside Callao on the Lima road are several small shipbuild-ing yards where the fishing smacks and other such small craft are built. At this time, however, there was little activity in the yards, as the fishing industry was in a depression—a far-reaching conse-quence of the hard European winter of 1962/3, which had held up stocks of fishmeal in the European ports. The result was a glut on the markets in the spring, bringing falling prices. Although the markets were, by June, getting back to normal, the fishing in-dustry was faced with another problem: the fish had disappeared. For several years the fish, mainly anchovies, had failed to disappear during the winter spawning season of May, June, and July. Instead of going to their spawning ground—the whereabouts of which is still a mystery—they had stayed in the fishing grounds. This failure to migrate coincided with a boom in the world fish-meal market, which the industry had met by treating the twelve-month season as if it had been normal. When prices temporarily fell—due to the sale of stocks accumulated in European ports— and fish simultaneously became scarce, due to a return to their normal migratory habits, many business men who had invested heavily in factories and boats found themselves in acute financial difficulties. Investments in progress, such as boats in the builders' yards, had to be halted; extensions of overdrafts and loans had to be sought, and finally the government was called in to treat fish-meal production as a temporarily depressed industry.

Beyond the shipyards came my first experience of the *barriadas*, the shanty-town slums that surround Lima. I had heard much about them and seen photographs brought back by the previous L.S.E. expedition. Even so, they came as a shock. At first I thought that what I saw stretching from the last boat-builder's yard up to the first of the few fields of corn, was a rubbish tip. Then a figure moved, and I realized that in fact it was an enormous number of square shacks made out of almost everything imaginable, with packing-cases, bamboo matting, and metal sheets predominating. The whole area was of the pervasive grey so characteristic of Lima. The narrow strips between the houses, that served as roads, were completely unpaved and were the only means of drainage as well as being the rubbish tip. I later discovered that this particular *barriada* was one of the worst, completely without lighting or health services, and with only a communal water supply. Later I was to learn more about life in the *barriadas*, visiting both those on the barren hills that surround Lima and those that are creeping into the desert. Some of the better established shanty-towns which the authorities have recognized, have more amenities; the older ones even have their own schools.

Driving into Lima at night from the desert proper, it is an eerie sight to see the faint street-lights of some of these districts edging up the hills. They culminate at a huge illuminated cross that dominates the skyline of Lima. Sometimes the cross can only be seen faintly through the seemingly eternal mist, and then the weak street-lights disappear. As one would expect, the mortality rate in these settlements is high, particularly among the children, who have not developed strength or cunning to survive the hardships. Disease is rampant. In the poorest districts the children's faces are covered with constantly running sores. They go about barefoot, or clad only in sandals made from pieces of car tyres.

But the taxi ran on, and soon we were passing the English cemetery with its strange above-ground vaults. Across the road from the cemetery were many flower-sellers displaying a rich variety of exotic blooms, all brought from higher up the valleys. For although Lima itself is covered with a blanket of thick depressing mist for almost eight months each year,* towns twenty-five miles inland have perpetual warm, brilliant sunlight. It was seeing such flowers that reminded me that the whole of Peru is in fact within the tropics.

---

* This is a result of its position at the meeting point of the cold Peruvian current and the prevailing easterly winds blowing off the warm land.

Lima: A City of Contrasts

Scattered on either side of the road were occasional farms, planted with food and raw materials for the Lima market. Cotton, vegetables, and sugar were evident, but the main crop was corn (maize). Rather tragically, these farms are being encroached on by the expanding city. Tragically, because this is the only area of fertile soil reasonably near Lima. A recent traveller* to Lima has described this area as a thriving industrial zone! The only evidence of industry that I can remember were a few sad factories and ware-houses forlornly lost in the rapidly rising housing estates.

The housing estates are impressive. The plan seems to be for the prospective estate-dweller to approach the development company for the estate in question, arrange a loan through them, and choose a plot of land on which the company then builds him an architect-designed house. This method of allowing each purchaser to choose his plot before the house is built, results in an untidy, piecemeal development. Until all the plots are taken, and all the houses built, the interim effect is that of a town after a blitz. But the estates—some consisting entirely of flats and maisonettes—are tidy and im-pressive as soon as all the sites are taken and building has ceased. Architects prosper in Lima. Even Peru's new President, Señor Belaúnde Terry, is an architect by profession. Furthermore, as its people are wont to boast, Lima has no rain; hence the houses need not be made weather-proof, which saves money in construction. The neat, well-designed, colourful housing estates were a sudden and dramatic contrast to the *barriadas* we had passed through earlier.

Entry into Lima is through an old decaying square, the junction of six roads leading out of the city through the suburbs into the desert. It is here that the Pan-American Highway meets the city. The houses in the square are tall and colonial; they have balconies and shutters, and their plaster façades are peeling away. They re-minded me of towns in northern Italy and northern Spain: so much so, that I began looking on the walls for shell and rifle-bullet scars. The route from this square to the Plaza San Martin,

* Michael Belthorpe writing in *Aspect* for June 1963.

the centre of Lima, is down the famous Avenida Colmena, with its soaring modern office blocks and fabulous hotels, especially the sky-scraping Hotel Crillon. The restaurant at the top of the Crillon building is known as the Skyroom, and the neon light that advertises it is among the landmarks of Lima, being visible out into the desert. My first entry into Lima was in twilight. The office blocks and hotels were ablaze with lights, and all the neon signs were aglow. The roads were choked with cars, their horns as usual at full blast. The pavements were filled with office workers and shop assistants on their way home. The whole place was alive.

Thus my first impression of Lima on the human side (gained from the taxi whilst we were searching for the hotel) was simply of bustling cosmopolitan crowds. The buildings, however, were continually providing surprises: a magnificent cathedral dating from the *Conquistadores* standing opposite a Woolworth type of supermarket; tiny little crumbling cafés next to towering bank offices; and well-preserved colonial houses contrasting with marble-faced hotels.

Soon after I had booked in at the hotel I was on my way to Miraflores (translated literally, Miraflores means Look! flowers), the favoured residential district which spread back from the sea. With two friends from the *Reina del Mar* I took a *collectivo* along the Avenida Arequipa, of which Lima dwellers are justifiably proud. They call it *la espina*—the backbone of Lima, for it runs down to the sea, and off it on both sides lie the older suburbs, like ribs. Along both it and its extension into the centre of Lima (Avenida Wilson) stand many fine buildings such as the Museum of Art, the Argentinean Embassy, and the Ministry of War. Along it too are some repulsive buildings, such as the American Embassy complete with Peruvian guards. Starting from Lima, the Avenue is at first lined with official buildings such as Ministries, Embassies, Museums, and the remains of the old Castle Prison. The next section passes through a number of parks filled with tropical trees and shrubs and, typically of Lima, statues; also, on every available bench, courting couples. Next comes a sector of oldish colonial houses, many turned into private schools. The mid-point between Lima and Miraflores is marked by a fly-over. From here to Miraflores stretch large blocks of modern luxury flats and modern architect-designed private houses, all different, and some converted into exclusive private schools, clinics, and cultural institutes. These ostentatious flats and houses come as something of a shock in contrast to the *barriadas* and housing estates. They were built because, until recently, the only means of making a substantial profit on private capital kept in Peru was by means of investment in real estate. For instance, one huge block of ultra-modern design is owned by a retired Chinese chemist. He is reputed to have made 500,000 dollars from his small chain of chemists' shops, and to have had this block of flats built when he retired, as a hedge against inflation and taxation.

The *collectivo* dropped us in the central square of Miraflores. Looking round us we could see, dominating the square, a fountain with floodlit water changing colours every few minutes. Behind us was the largest block of flats we had so far seen, built—almost entirely of glass—over some modern shops, restaurants, bars, and a cinema. The square was a shopping centre, brightly lit by neon signs and lights. On the far side of the green square was a church, and a little beyond it a bowling alley.

This ostentatious display of wealth is by no means confined to the residential and amenity districts. I was to meet it continuously during the next two weeks, as I tramped from office to office in search of the 'Open Sesame' document that would release our crates from the Callao Customs.

I had been warned to expect some difficulty with the Peruvian Customs and was prepared with a sheaf of special permits and orders. I had to work quickly if I was to be in Chiquian with the crates before the main party arrived. My attempts to do so, however, were successfully frustrated by the combined efforts of the obstinate and inefficient customs officials, and of our agent's chronic inertia. When I rang the agent, the morning after my arrival, he told me that it would be a few days before the crates were cleared. When I asked why, he replied that the problem lay in the need to collect all the required signatures on one and the same day. And *that* was difficult, because somebody was always missing from his office.

Each morning I would ring the agent from my hotel, and each morning would be told the same tale. Today his clerk had been unable to find some official or other, but tomorrow, he always assured me, he was sure that they would be successful. Pete Bebbington had warned me about the Peruvian *mañana* which never came, and so I resigned myself to a long wait. None of my suggestions for getting round the problem were thought feasible. The clerk was too busy to wait in an official's office for his return. No, it was not possible to see the officials by appointment. And no, it was not possible for me to go down myself. But I was not to worry, tomorrow the crates would be released.

Pete Bebbington had also told me that if I ran into trouble with the customs I should contact Caeser Morales Arnao. As President of the *Club Andino Peruano*, Señor Morales is a well-known figure in the mountaineering world; he also holds the government post of Director of Andeanism, which entitles him to an office in the Ministry of Education. All foreign expeditions to Peru that have passed through Lima since Señor Morales was appointed to his position in the Ministry, have written in warm terms of the help he gave to them in negotiating the terrors of the customs. So after I had wasted a few days hanging around I decided to ask Morales for his help. I had no difficulty in finding his office, for the skyscraping Ministry of Education building is the most dominant on the Lima skyline. It is an imposing building of twenty-four floors, but despite its outward impressiveness it hides an unbelievably inefficient institution. Even when I managed to find Morales' office nobody there would admit to having heard of him. Several telephone calls within the Ministry eventually uncovered the fact that he seldom came into this office as he had another one across town. Nobody knew *why* he had this other office, but I supposed it to be due to his frustration with the great Ministry building.

I rang his other office and was answered by his sister, who told me that Caeser was out of town. He was organizing a mountaineering conference in Huaraz and would not be back for a week. I began to feel that I was cornered, and in desperation went on a tour of the relevant Ministries in search of someone who could authorize the immediate release of the equipment. In my roamings, I discovered that the Ministry of Education building is typical of the current trend in office architecture in Lima. It is difficult to see any sound reasons behind such expensive structures. There is no apparent gain in space, and the capital and labour used in building them could obviously be used to greater social advantage. There would be some excuse if the larger and more impressive buildings brought about any increase in efficiency. Efficiency, however, depends upon the man, not on the building he works in.

Another example of chronic inefficiency within a modern building is the Ministry of Finance, although this is slightly less pretentious than the Ministry of Education. I would not be surprised to hear that the Ministry of Finance building has collapsed under the weight of the paper that it houses. Its offices were so full of paper that I was reminded of the Brazilian film, *Black Orpheus*, in which such a building, with its rooms and corridors overflowing with paper, is used as a symbol of Hell. Not that the amount of paper proves the efficiency of the organization: it is caused merely by the profusion of tax laws. I believe that there are several thousand identifiable forms for the Peruvian tax-payer to worry over. There is also an abundance of documents and permits which need validating by a Treasury official. The consequential chaos is Heaven for the petty bureaucrat and Hell indeed for the citizen. Or it would be, if the average Peruvian was worried by such things. Yet, as one example shows, it would not be very difficult

c

to improve the working of the system. In the Ministry of Finance, at the tax-payer's expense, a hired computer has been installed, complete with all subsidiary machines and a trained staff. This installation is competent to keep records of all items of government revenue and expenditure. Indeed, it is more than competent to maintain such accounts: it already has the necessary information and is ready—at the push of a button—to prepare figures both for all direct taxes and for all duties paid on exports and imports. So far, however, the powers that be have not deigned to use it. Nor is it difficult to see the reason. For, with a separate card for each tax-payer, records would be really accurate and completely fool-proof—which is the last thing the officials want.

This specific example of potential progress is rejected, because the only people who could authorize its use are just the people who would stand to lose by the reform. A substantial proportion of taxes (85% in the case of some) are paid without any individual record being made. The assessment is personal and arbitrary and the assessor can be bribed into under-assessing. This tragi-comic way of organizing a Ministry of Finance produces statistics that are completely useless as a basis for planning or for any other economic assessment. For example, in the National Income Statistics for 1956 the Government is shown as having raised more than half its income from a category of tax-payers called 'Others'. This is tantamount to admitting: 'We have so much money in the Treasury: we have no idea where more than half of it came from, and we don't *want* to know. But at least we have it.' Any attempt to describe Lima and its ways must frankly recognize that corruption and patronage are commonplaces.

Personal impressions of Lima depend on how one's time is spent there, and on those with whom one spends it. Most English and American descriptions of the city read as though they had been written by someone who had never left the *émigré* colony, and whose opinions were formed in one of the many club bars. Life can be good, very good, for a foreigner in Lima. He need feel no qualms of conscience about the acute poverty and distress. Moving in circles well above subsistence-level, he will think—if, indeed, he gives it a thought—that Peru's problems are not his.

One man who lived in voluntary exile in Lima put it to me thus: 'Everyone would be better off if the Indians just stayed in the hills.' The same man said that, in his opinion, more than foreign capital was needed to develop Peru: two or three hundred-thousand West European immigrants would be required to 'get things going and then keep them going'. The Peruvian Indian, he thought, is worn out, devoid of initiative or drive, and un-educable beyond a certain elementary level. Such an attitude does not allow the Peruvian much room or future in his own country.

An intensely patriotic young professional man denounced as treason the growing tendency among the young to leave Peru, simply to increase their personal wealth, after they had been trained at Peruvian universities, colleges or institutes. At this point we realized suddenly that we had been talking at cross-purposes; for he was using 'Peru' to mean simply Lima, whereas I was referring to the whole, huge, diverse country. 'Peru ends at the outskirts of Lima,' he said. To which I answered: 'Surely that's where Peru begins?'

These two conversations suggest that many people in Lima regard the city as a self-contained, self-sufficient unit, accidentally attached to a country called Peru. Yet the basic problems are those of Peru, not Lima. Lima has in itself no problem of poverty; it is a thriving, industrious, advanced community. It is the Indians who bring poverty down with them from their mud-huts in the Andes. Most of the better-off members of Lima society refuse to recognize the Indians' poverty as a national problem, and are quite happy to take you to the *barriadas* to see how these miserable 'Peruvians' live. The abject poverty of the *barriadas* has become one of the tourist show-pieces of Lima.

While I was engaged in my perambulations of Lima, the main

party arrived. They flew in on a night plane from Miami and were surprised to find me waiting for them at the airport, together with a group of the *Club Andino Peruano* which had come to welcome the party to Peru.

It was good to see others from the expedition, for after a month on my own I was beginning to feel isolated. Vic was the first to appear through the barrier: characteristically, he had not bothered to wait for his passport to be checked, but had somehow found a way past the inspectors. He was carrying some mail for me from England, which I read while we waited for the others to filter through the authorities and while Vic renewed his friendship with the *Club Andino*. It was half an hour before the other four were out. Graham and Charlie were first, followed by Dave Condict and Pete Westnidge. Despite the effects of four days' continuous travel, Dave looked as though he were off to speech day at Dulwich College. Pete was more in character, looking as if he had just come off the rocks at Stanage. Graham was, as usual, detached and nonchalant, his only interest being to get to bed as soon as possible.

We piled into two cars and drove off to the hotel which Pete Bebbington had recommended, and which I had by now found. I left them there, and went back to my own hotel. If they had been surprised to find me waiting for them at the airport, they were even more surprised by leaving me—the supposed 'advance party'—behind them, when they left Lima for Chiquian three days later. There was no point in anyone else waiting in Lima, wasting our limited funds on hotel bills, so they were moving up to Chiquian—with a case of food that I had brought—to begin acclimatizing. They were also taking over from me the responsibility of looking for *burros* and enquiring about the best route in to Rondoy. No progress had been made with the customs, and I resigned myself to more boredom and frustration.

Early in the morning after the main party's departure, I was awakened by the telephone. The hall porter was ringing to tell me that a Mr Farrell was on his way up to my room. Before I had time to dress or to work out what other plane he could have come on, the door opened, and in stormed Pete Farrell, a flat-cap pulled well down over his forehead.

'Watcha me old tater,' he greeted me.

'Er, hello, I take it you're Pete Farrell,' I replied, a little put out by having to introduce myself dressed only in string vest and ankle socks.

'S'right. I know you're Dave Wall, the porter told me. Where are the others?'

As I pulled my trousers on, I explained the customs situation, and how the main party was on its way to Chiquian. He knew our agent, and gave me his—forthright—opinions of the man's abilities. I agreed. I brewed some foul coffee from hot tap-water while he explained his arrival at this unexpected time. On disembarking at Panama he had found that there had been a mix-up over his plane tickets, and he had had to switch to the New York/Buenos Aires jet, paying a surcharge. He had no idea when he arrived whether any of us were in Lima, and had automatically come to the Claridge Hotel, where he had stayed with the New Zealand expedition the year before.

The telephone rang while we were talking: it was Señor Morales. He had arrived back in Lima that morning and, hearing of the problem we were facing, was on his way round. While we waited Pete Farrell had a shower and I went out for a bottle of rum to wash away the disgusting taste of tap-water coffee. Señor Morales turned out to be a teetotaller, so it was just Pete and I who drank, while I repeated the tale of what had been happening since I arrived. This was quite easy, as nothing *had* happened. Morales, apparently annoyed, immediately rang the agent. After a few minutes heated and animated conversation he replaced the receiver and told us that the crates would be cleared in the morning. I tried not to laugh.

The following morning the crates really were released. This took us by surprise. After searching Lima for a lorry, we eventually located the transport firm that ran a service to Chiquian. The owner of the firm was sorry, he told us, but all his lorries were out of Lima. He thought, though, that we might perhaps have one on the following day for £20. We realized that, in Peruvian style, he was really asking us how much extra we were prepared to pay to get a lorry that day. So we offered him 25% more. Sure enough, he rang back a few minutes later with the news that a lorry had just happened to pull into the garage. Where did we want it to pick us up? We gave him the address, and a few hours later we were busy loading. In doing so we discovered that three crates were missing. One contained four new ice-axes, the others a dozen bottles of gin each. We could afford to lose the gin, but the absence of the ice-axes was serious. We left a note for Pete Bebbington with Señor Morales, telling him of the missing axes, and set off at five from the hotel, *en route* for Chiquian. Or so we thought.

First we had to collect the documents for the journey, and then the driver's wife. She was to accompany us with a box of pullets to sell in the Andean villages. Even after this the driver seemed loathe to leave the city, and it was nine-thirty before we reached the outskirts where another stop occurred at the check-point on the Pan-American Highway. And while we waited for the driver to have his documents checked I looked back to Lima.

Lima: the grey city. A city with an introspective population leading vigorous lives. Enthusiastically proud of the city and its history, they are fully active in its present, and exuberantly confident in its future. A city of desperate poverty, glossed over with immense riches; a developing city, capital of an under-developed, half forgotten country. I was glad to be leaving, after thirteen days of frustrating delay: it was a wonderful feeling to be out, and on the final stretch of the journey to Rondoy. But I knew that I was also looking forward to my return.

A few miles past the check-point we stopped again, twice: once for a meal, and the second time for the driver to say his prayers and light a candle at a wayside shrine for travellers—a custom, he told us, observed by long-distance drivers.

Fifty miles from Lima we reached the Pasomayo, a stretch of road cut into a sand-cliff sheering away into the Pacific. Now I felt that at last the expedition had really begun. The tension that I had built up in the months of preparation, in London and in Lima, suddenly released. Exhausted, I dug my down-jacket out of the crates and fell asleep on the back of the lorry. The only thought in my mind was that at last we were on our way to Rondoy.

2

Peru: From Lima to Chiquian

An old student of the London School of Economics, Victor Raúl Haya de la Torre, is at present leader of the opposition in the Peruvian Chamber of Deputies (his party: the American Popular Revolutionary Alliance). He has said that to travel across Peru is to travel through all the stages of civilization. Even our short journey of 300 miles or so, from Lima to the village where our mule trek to the Cordillera Huayhuash would begin, took us from the highly sophisticated, westernized Lima to the communities of coca-chewing* Indians, while leading us through a wide variation of geographical features. Peru is no more than a political unit. It has no unity in its people, who vary in race from the savage tribes of the Amazon jungle, through the Andean and *Altiplano* Indian descendants of the Incas, to the modern city-dwellers of Lima. Geographically, Peru is split up into three distinct regions and numerous sub-regions, with the minimum of communication between them.

On our lorry ride from Lima to Chiquian, Pete Farrell and I passed through two of the main regions, and from the second we could see the third. We travelled up at night and were only able to fill in the visual details later, on our return journey.

After leaving Lima the Pan-American Highway follows the coast, and we went with it for 150 miles or so before we turned inland. It came as something of a surprise to me to find that we were in the middle of a desert almost as soon as we left Lima. This

---

* The leaves of the *coca* bush chewed together with a few drops of lime-essence release cocaine. Most Peruvian Indians are addicted to cocaine, its effects enable them to endure the privations forced upon them by their environment.

26

1. Looking down to Chiquian from the road

2. Chiquian main street

3. Peter Bebbington

4. Graham Sadler

5. David Condict

6. Charles Powell

7. David Wall

8. Vic Walsh

9. Peter Westnidge

10. Peter Farrell

11. Town Square, Queropalca

12. Shop courtyard, Queropalca. Strips of meat can be seen hanging to dry on the line, out of the reach of dogs

desert stretches some 2,000 miles, from the Equator to thirty degrees south. It is produced by the winds that blow from off the land onto the sea. These winds have lost all their rain by the time they have crossed the Andes. No rain falls along the coastal strip. The sand-desert that runs from the south of Peru into Chile—the Atacama Desert—is the driest in the world, running right down into the sea. The sea-side resort for the Lima aristocracy, Ancon, is a fantastic collection of mammoth blocks of luxury flats built literally in the middle of the desert. In the winter it is a ghost town; for there is no work except for those who, during the hot summer months, provide services for the flat-owners and day-visitors. Other features of the desert near Lima were the development towns; to make one of these, a road had simply been blazed into the desert, and, at the end of it, prefabricated houses and factories had been erected with all services laid on. They were built to absorb some of the surplus population from Lima, and I suspect that a similar intention lay behind the founding of a children's settlement, a walled-in compound with chalet-like buildings isolated in the desert. Such 'Children's Towns', to be found all over South America, are provided for the unwanted children of the slums, and are always sited well away from the cities' consciences.

The road itself has its spectacular stretches, the most impressive being the Pasomayo. Whereas the coastal strip is for the most part a plain, at this one point the road has to cut its way round a series of steep sand-cliffs, which drop away hundreds of feet to the sea below. Seeing, for the first time, the waves crashing below and the sand-cliffs soaring overhead, I was startled into admiration.

The desert is not continuous, for the desert sand is very fertile when irrigated. Irrigation projects have brought into cultivation a million-and-a-quarter acres, which constitute the major agricultural region in Peru. A wide variety of crops are grown, although sugar and other canes, rice, and cotton predominate. These artificial, man-made oases became trouble-spots while we were in

Peru. For most of the irrigation projects are privately owned, and it is typical to find a fenced-in area of luxurious farm-land on one side of the road, while on the other is a settlement of poor Indians, eking out a living from the desert. These desert Indians live in appalling conditions, building their houses from canes and driftwood.

The use of land is *the* unsettled question in Peru. All the political parties have plans for agrarian reform. Earlier in the year, during the elections, it had been the main plank in the platforms of all three presidential candidates. This competition has made the issue an acute embarrassment for the winner of those elections, President Fernando Belaúnde Terry, who, in an attempt to gain popular support, had promised the Indians sweeping agrarian reforms. The Indians have waited a long time. In the past, hunger has driven them to invade and squat on the huge estates, often badly cultivated by absentee landlords. The automatic answer to such squatting was to send a highly armed squad of soldiers to shoot the 'trespassers'. The unsophisticated Indians took Belaúnde's election promises to mean that if he were elected the land would become theirs. And sure enough, about a month after he took office, the Indians—starting in the south where there are allegedly Cuba-trained 'communist insurgents'—began to invade the *haciendas* in large numbers. To send in troops was an impossible solution both because of Belaúnde's commitment and because of the number of Indians involved. Nor could he accept the situation as a *fait accompli*. For he is astute enough to realize that simply to give each Indian family a small piece of land would be a backward step in economic development; and, furthermore, he is not sufficiently strong, politically speaking, to ignore the pressure-group of rich landowners. He was still seeking a solution to this problem when we left Peru.

Along the coast, too, are several small towns based on the fishing industry, with modern fishmeal plants; these towns can be distinguished, even at night, by their characteristic smell!

Peru: From Lima to Chiquian

After 150 miles or so, just beyond the town of Barranca, our road branched off the Pan-American Highway and turned sharply inland. Immediately we entered a different part of the coastal area; from the coast proper (*costa baja*) we moved into what the Peruvians call the 'coast's eyebrow' (*ceja de costa*). The dun-coloured sand of the desert gave way to thick grey dust, covering a plain a few miles wide which led up to the *costa alta* (high coast). This plain is completely barren, covered with dust and rubble. Occasional patches of rock moss, fed by the sea fogs, are the only plant life. The road led into a steep-sided, narrowing river valley, and began to mark the boundary between the rubble-covered hillsides and the cultivated river valley. The river had virtually dried up when we passed in early July, but in the rain season, from October to April, it becomes the lifeline for the settlements that cultivate, along the banks of the river, sugar and other canes, oranges, and other surprisingly exotic plants. As the road began to climb more steeply we left behind us the overcast skies, and emerged into bright moonlight. In daytime it would have been into the burning sun.

Dawn that morning brought no exciting views, only the rubble-covered hillsides, with an occasional cactus plant. Here and there an early Indian farmer was up and irrigating his little potato plot from a water-can strapped to his back, or ploughing by hand with a primitive wooden plough. The image is strong in my mind, of waking that morning to find desolation on all sides, with cacti prodding up the dust, and an occasional peasant struggling for an existence: the whole effect was accentuated by lorry loads of poor Indians with their bundles, which now and then passed us on their way down to the coast.

These lorry loads of Indians converge on the coastal settlements, especially the shanty-town *barriadas* of Lima, from all parts of Peru. It is as if the whole population of the Sierra and high plains are sliding down to the coast under the simple force of gravity. Some are repelled by the hunger and deprivation of their homes;

others are attracted by the greater opportunities for work and education, or just for city life. Every year tens of thousands of these people leave the homes of their ancestors, lured to the 'city'. Although Peru has one of the world's highest birth rates, the population of the Sierra is continually decreasing. No census data exist for the Sierra, of course; but the population of the Lima/Callao area, an estimated 650,000 in 1940, is now over two million. The percentage of women involved in this migration is greater than that of men. This is because all urban households, down to the lowest levels of wage labourers, employ house servants. In the Sierra villages it is unusual to come across women between the ages of about thirteen to forty. When, around eight o'clock that morning, we stopped for breakfast, our eggs and coffee were cooked for us by women of about sixty, and served to us by little girls of eight or nine.

In the village—a sleepy, dusty place, reminiscent of a Yugoslav border town—we filled some cans with paraffin: at least, our driver did it for us, sucking on a tube from a large drum to siphon it into the little cans that we had brought from Lima as security against a can shortage in Chiquian. The driver miscalculated and swallowed a huge mouthful of the crude liquid, to the amusement of the lethargic Indians who had gathered to watch the strange *gringo's* antics. It turned out later that these efforts were wasted, there being a shortage neither of cans nor of paraffin at Chiquian.

After breakfast, as we were setting off from the police checkpoint, we took on what I thought at first was a police escort. In fact we were just giving him a lift to a point a few miles up the valley where someone was waiting for him with a horse, on which he galloped off up the hillside. The valley was greener now, with eucalyptus trees dotted around. Farms and settlements were now much more in evidence; so were (illegal) political slogans on the hillsides and on house-walls, in favour of Haya de la Torre, whose strongest support is in this area. The road, too, was taking on more of the character I expected of an Andean road. Hugging the hillsides, with the slopes dropping away beneath us for hundreds of feet, it zig-zagged backwards and forwards, gaining height continuously.

The custom prevails of placing a cross at points in the road where drivers have taken corners too sharply, fallen asleep while driving, or lost control, and in consequence have plummeted over into the ravine. There can be no hope for anyone who does go over, and the number of crosses is frightening. Driving along this road on the back of an uncovered lorry, behind a Peruvian driver, was a testing experience; from time to time I found myself hoping that the candle lit in the shrine at the start of our journey had not gone out.

Later on, when the sun reached its zenith and peak heat, and we were beginning to feel the effects of the rapidly gained altitude, we stopped at one of the many roadside bars. This was like others of its type, being built on a platform level with the road—a knob of earth that formed something of a natural platform sloping down steeply from the road, that the Indians had levelled with *adobe* building blocks. At this point I should perhaps explain that I have so far been using the word 'Indian', indiscriminately, to refer to anyone who is not 'white Peruvian': in fact the Peruvians, like all other peoples, stratify themselves very carefully. The Peruvian classes consist of: whites, *mestizos* (mixed race), Indians, Yellows, Negroes, and, according to the Ministry of Finance, 'not declared'. The social ordering is strictly adhered to, and people are offended if they are wrongly classified. For example, at this bar where we stopped for a beer and to water the chickens, the owner and his family were proudly *mestizos*. He was having an extension built to his *adobe* shack, and the builder's labourers were pure-bred Indians; they were all middle- to old-aged, and their overseer, a youth of about eighteen, was a *mestizo*.

We arrived during their lunch hour, which for the Indians consisted solely of coca-chewing and spirit-drinking. Outside the towns a few leaves of coca usually form a major part of the

Indian's pay packet, along with a quantity of alcohol, and very little money. In Peru one often hears of Indians being paid less than sixpence a week (for comparison, a street cleaner in Lima will normally earn 18/6 a week). As we went into the bar, the foreman came out, and as soon as he appeared the Indians set to work. We welcomed the cool, shaded interior, after the hot sun outside. The only things that seemed to be on sale were pilsen-type beer, and the inevitable cola drinks—the usual Coca-Cola and Pepsi; the Peruvian colas such as Inca Cola; and another which amused us for its ability to turn up in the most unlikely places, called Cola Inglese, that is, English Cola. Why 'English' nobody seemed to know. We bought some beers and went out to watch the builders working with *adobe*. They used dry mud blocks, about fifteen inches by eight inches by six inches; for scaffolding, they used planks balanced on the walls already laid. As the binding material was freshly-mixed mud, each block had to be laid rapidly before the sun had dried it.

The chickens were packed back in their box and we climbed aboard for the last stage, over the *Puna* to Chiquian. As the lorry climbed up from the bar, the scenery became more like a piedmont region. After a couple of hours the green of arable farming on the terraced hillsides and the valley floor began to give way to pasture, grazed by stringier cows and goat-like sheep. Higher still the animals began to thin out, and the vegetation was reduced to a tough grass—*puna* grass. At about 14,000 feet the slope suddenly eased off and we found ourselves on the *Puna*, the high plateau region found on both sides of the Andes.

Pete Farrell and I began to feel the effects of *sorroche*, the altitude sickness that results from the body's failure to adapt itself rapidly enough to the sudden lack of oxygen. The party that had gone on ahead of us had suffered no ill effects from crossing the *Puna*, before descending into the Chiquian valley. In their saloon car they had crossed the high altitude area much more comfortably and with less fatigue than we did on the open back of the comparatively slow lorry. We attempted to drown the effects by drinking the remains of the beer; but the only result was to make us so drowsy that we both lay on top of the crates and fell asleep. An hour or so later I stretched and stood up, leaning on the driver's cab. Straight ahead, on the horizon beyond the *Puna*, was a magnificent snow-covered peak; at that moment it was Nirvana itself to me. The Cordillera Huayhuash actually in sight! In my excitement I mistook it for Rondoy, though later—as the rest of the high ridge came into view—I realized that it must have been Rondoy's neighbour, Jirishanca. Looking round, I saw that the character of the *Puna* had changed; it was now something like an enormous Scottish moor, with a springy, hard grass. Small pools abounded, surrounded by bog, since there was no drainage system to take away the melt-water of the previous winter's snows. Now, in early July, it was cold and windy, and the occasional patch of snow still persisted. The seasons are reversed up here, for Lima has its summer from January to April, when the sea fogs disperse, uncovering the overhead sun. In the Andean region and on the *Puna* and *Altiplano* the winter comes in the rain season, October to March, when the thick clouds blot out the heat of the sun and the rain falls as snow and hail.

Due north lay the Cordillera Blanca, with the towering summit of Huascarán, at 22,180 feet the second highest mountain in South America. The flatness of the intervening plateau gave a false impression of closeness, making the snow-covered foothills of the Blanca seem but a few miles away, when in fact the distance was some sixty miles.

We stopped for a few minutes in a tiny village near where the road forked—due north to Huaraz, the main town in the Blanca region, and straight on for Chiquian. The village was very primitive, though we noticed one of the well-marked football pitches which are found throughout Peru. Of the twenty or so buildings, four were 'business premises', closed as usual—they only open if a customer presents himself. The four businesses were: the police station, the government coca shop, a general store, and the inevitable party office of the *Apristas* (Haya de la Torre's American Popular Revolutionary Alliance). I asked about the coca shop and discovered that, owing to its importance in the Indian economy, the production of coca and its distribution is a government monopoly. Control, however, is ineffective, and most coca is produced, distributed, and consumed illegally.

As we travelled across the *Puna*, the whole of the high central ridge of the Huayhuash came into view. At first I was a little puzzled, until I realized that most of the photographs that I had seen were taken from the other side. Then I was able to recognize the grand peak of Yerupaja, 21,560 feet, towering above the rest of the ridge; next came Yerupaja Chico, then the twin-peaked Jirishanca—and, at the end, the mountain we had crossed the world for: Rondoy.

The Cordillera Huayhuash is one of the shortest ranges in the Andes, being only some twenty miles long; and yet it is probably the most magnificent in Peru. The two neighbouring ranges, the Cordilleras Blanca and Raura (the scene of the L.S.E. expedition in 1961) are both much longer. The three ranges are not part of a continuous chain, but arranged in a staggered order: the Blanca in the north-west: the central Huayhuash fifty miles or so east and south of the Blanca; and the Raura to the south-east again. The zones between the three ranges are completely free of glaciers and permanent snow.

The Cordillera Huayhuash is the focal point of the continental watershed. From the melt-waters of its glaciers is formed the River Marañon which, one and a half thousand miles further on at Iquitos, becomes the Amazon. From the ridges of the Huayhuash the view one way is across the *Puna* to the coast, and on the other across the rolling foothills to the Amazon jungle.

Soon the road began its hair-raising descent into the Chiquian valley. It had to zig-zag down the steep side of the *Puna*, the apexes of the zigs and zags being sharp hairpin bends, usually

13. Base Camp

14. Rondoy (*left*) and Ninashanca; with ice-face, ice-basin, and ice-fall in upper centre. The route started in the lower section, from base camp, which is behind the dark patch in lower right, and followed the moraine leading up to left centre, above the lake. From there, more or less directly up to the level of the ice-basin and then traverse right

marked with crosses! We travelled miles for every hundred feet descended. And as we descended, the land was becoming cultivated again, the slopes being terraced. Pete Farrell noticed the sun catching the rooftops of a settlement across the valley which we took to be Chiquian. But a few miles further on we turned a corner and, a thousand or so feet below us, saw what was obviously the town. It was still several miles of road away.

From above, Chiquian looks as though it has been laid out for a gigantic crossword puzzle. The streets are symmetrically arranged at right-angles, the symmetry broken only by the town's several squares. As we came nearer, the streets began to look so unbelievably narrow that, when we came into the main square, I bet Pete that the road the driver was 'aiming' his lorry at would be too narrow for us to pass through. I lost my bet. The driver seemed to know where to take us, and a few hundred feet down the street he pulled up in front of the Hotel Santa Rosa. We were immediately surrounded by hoards of children, pointing at us and shouting 'gringo', 'hello', and 'good-bye'. Pete Farrell disappeared into the hotel and brought out Charlie, Vic, and Dave Condict. They told us that Pete Westnidge and Graham had gone off on a reconnaissance of the route. As we unloaded, the lorry driver's wife unpacked her chickens and began to hawk them to the Indians who had gathered to see what we were unloading. As soon as we had carried the crates into the hotel and stacked them in the room which the hotel owner was lending us, Pete Farrell and I lay down, both of us suffering from *sorroche* headaches.

When the main party had arrived on the Monday, July 1st, three days earlier, they were expecting me to turn up the following day. As a slip in organization had left them with little money, they were unable to start hiring the mules. So, partly to save money and partly owing to our lack of maps, Pete Westnidge and Graham had set off on the Tuesday to reconnoitre the route into the Huayhuash. As all their gear was still in Lima, they were forced to walk in baseball boots, and neither of them had airbeds. They carried packs of 35 lb and, being completely unacclimatized, found the going hard. Pete in particular was breathing badly, having to gasp for breath on the steep stretches.

The path leading out of Chiquian towards the Huayhuash forked after a few miles. Pete Bebbington, on his earlier visit, had taken the right fork. This led to a small village called Pacclon and then up to the glacial lakes immediately below the south-east face of Rondoy. Our first problem was to find out if this was also the best route round to the other side of Rondoy, where we should be climbing. Bonatti had mentioned the villages of Llamac and Popca, which lay along the other fork. Pete Westnidge and Graham were hoping to find which of the paths leading to the passes across the Andean ridge involved the least effort and shortest distance.

They told us later that they had taken the right fork, leading to Pacclon. As they neared the village the path steepened abruptly. And as they struggled up the last thirty yards a crowd of Indian children appeared above them and began to shower them with stones. They were very appreciative of this kind gesture. They fought their way through the reception committee to the local shop, where they were amazed to find Pepsi-Cola on sale. The shop had been opened in their honour and, as they drank, the whole village turned out to watch them, gazing in amazement. The children fought amongst themselves to touch our advance party who, disturbed by their popularity, left the village in search of a bivouac site. Further up the track, near a bridge, they found some flat ground where they settled down for the night, being joined at supper by a wandering violin-player.

The next morning they followed the track to the top of a ridge. Pete found the going hard, having to stop every twenty yards to catch his breath, but Graham was going quite well. At the top Pete calculated that they were about 600 feet higher than

Mont Blanc and began to feel better. They descended by the alternative route to Popca where they spent the second night. They were now at a loss for their next move, not knowing what was happening in Chiquian. Fortunately for us they decided to return, having discovered that the route via Pacclon was a lengthy and ardous detour. They made good time back to Chiquian although they found the last few miles, up a steep track, desperately hard. My favourite sick joke of the expedition is the picture of the two of them straining up the hill to Chiquian, both worrying about their lack of fitness. Near the top, a few hundred yards from the town, an Indian passed them. He had heard that we were intending big things in the Huayhuash, and cynically asked: 'Yerupaja? Huh?', and went off chuckling to himself. The rumour had spread around Chiquian that we were intending to climb Yerupaja—the highest peak in the Huayhuash—and seeing the difficulty that Pete and Graham were encountering in simply walking up the (to him) slight gradient, he held little hope for us on the mountain!

They arrived at the hotel to find Pete Farrell and me lying on our beds, our heads buried in pillows to muffle the shattering noise of boxes being opened. We brewed up and listened to their tales of the dreaded *sorroche*. Graham had had difficulty in digesting food and had been vomiting the night before. But worst of all was Pete's account of how he had found it impossible to smoke more than three cigarettes a day, and those only while sitting absolutely still!

We 'dined' around the corner in the village restaurant, on the famous Peruvian *sopa a la minuta*, a brew containing everything happening to be at hand when the water in the pot starts to boil. Having come across some pretty poor versions of this dish in Lima, we were a little suspicious when we found that it was the only item on the menu. It went down quite well, however, and we sat on afterwards yarning about our separate journeys: Pete Farrell's from New Zealand, the main party's across the States, and mine in the *Reina del Mar*. We provided entertainment for, it seemed, the entire population of Chiquian. They crowded the door in an attempt to see the *gringos*. We were told tales of all the other expeditions that had passed that way *en route* for the Huayhuash, especially the German one, two of whom had fallen through a crevasse to their deaths. We were to be told this story many times in Chiquian. The wonderful old lady who kept the café provided us with music from the B.B.C.'s Latin American service on her transistor radio. Her husband amused himself by watching our reactions to the little sips of strong *pisco* (the local spirit) which he gave to each of us. It took some effort to leave the cosy gaslit room for the night outside.

Although cold, it was a beautiful moonlit night, and we wandered to the edge of the town, escorted by dozens of little Indian children, with the three words '*gringo*', 'hello', and 'good-bye', constantly on their lips. At the edge of the village we stood and looked across the intervening valleys to the peaks of the Cordillera Huayhuash, our eyes converging on the silvered peak of Rondoy. It seemed so close now, after all the months of preparation. Mumbling something about the cold, we shuffled back to the hotel, each lost in his own thoughts.

At the hotel we found the town's muleteers waiting to quote us for the trek to base camp. They stated a completely ridiculous price, which the hotel-keeper told us would be enough to buy the *burros* outright. Nobody being in an argumentative mood, we told them to come back in the morning. Then we sent word to the English-speaking schoolteacher (the one responsible for the children's 'hellos' and 'good-byes') asking him to come round in the morning to help us with the language problem.

The night itself provided some entertainment. I was woken in the dead of night by the noise of a bed shaking, but put it down to someone fighting in the next room. Then I realized that it was my own bed that was shaking, and not only mine, but all the beds in the room. The room itself was shaking! Then the whole animal population of Chiquian began to howl and squawk. We were having an earthquake.

We later discovered that, at that exact moment, Pete Bebbington had just passed through the immigration control at Lima-Callao airport; he recognized the first signs of the tremor and left the building quickly. A few seconds later, as the tremor reached its peak (its centre was the Callao area and it was quite strong at the airport), the windows of the airport buildings shattered, and cracks appeared in the walls. The people inside scrambled for the doors in a panic, but nobody was hurt.

It lasted only a few minutes and soon everything was quiet again in Chiquian. But not for long. I awoke again to find Pete Westnidge standing in the middle of the room turning his sleeping-bag inside out, convinced that it contained one of Chiquian's famous *pulgas*, a sort of outsize flea. Although he turned the light on, he failed to find it and returned to bed, disgruntled.

3

Chiquian to Base Camp

We were rudely awakened the next morning by Adrian, the young orphan protégé of the hotel-keeper, shouting to us that the *arrieros* had arrived to discuss our arrangements. Over coffee, the *arrieros* told us that they themselves were at that time the only muleteers with any animals in Chiquian. This information was obviously intended to warn us that their price was still likely to be high. It was. They explained that they had only fifteen or sixteen donkeys, which would mean that two trips would be necessary. The schoolteacher, who had just arrived to translate for us, confirmed their story that the other pack-animals usually to be found in Chiquian were away at a big market. Even so we thought their price was too high and decided to bargain.

They began by asking for 8,000 *soles* (the current rate of the *sole* was 75 to the £1) and refused to bargain. They sat motionless, only occasionally attempting to justify their price. We were equally adamant. We had to be, as our total assets at the time were 5,000 *soles*. We offered them 4,000. They laughed. We shrugged our shoulders and left them. Then we started to unpack the crates, breaking everything down into loads for the *burros*. After talking amongst themselves, the muleteers approached us with a new offer of 6,000 *soles*. They chose a bad time, as we had just discovered that one of the large tins of honey had been leaking disastrously. To add to the confusion, Ted, the schoolteacher, had had to leave us to prepare for the fiesta that the schoolteachers were organizing for the following day. We offered 5,000 *soles*, with such conviction that they immediately walked out. We were not unduly worried, knowing that even if *they* had the only *burros* in Chiquian,

40

we were the only expedition there to hire them; and we guessed that, even at our price, we could find animals in neighbouring towns ready to make the trek.

It turned out that we were right; for as soon as the muleteers left the hotel, the landlord, who had all the time stayed in the background, came across and told us that he knew a man in a little village some miles away who would be able to find us *burros*. He took us to Señor Alvarez, the local commercial genius. Alvarez thought he could probably meet our needs for 4,800 *soles*. We now experienced some of his astuteness, for he refused to set off to collect the mules unless we gave him an advance of 10%, and also the cost of the hire of his horse. After a morning of continuous bargaining in the hot sun we were all rather strained and suspicious at the prospect of parting with a tenth of our assets to Alvarez, who, we all agreed, looked decidedly shifty. Fortunately, at this point Ted arrived with an invitation to the fiesta and a recommendation of Alvarez. We were still a bit suspicious, but Ted persuaded Alvarez to give us a receipt, and, satisfied by this, we gave him the money and he set off for Popca.

After an exhausting afternoon, breaking down the loads for the mules, we went round to the little café for dinner. They had killed a chicken for us and made a soup of it. To do full justice to the meal we sent out for a crate of ale. Someone mentioned that they had found a billiard hall in the main square and off we set, escorted as usual by a score or so of screeching Indian children. A little perturbed to find that the Peruvian billiard table has no pockets but enormous balls, we played a few games and returned to the café, where we sent out for another crate of ale. Eventually all available supplies of ale ran out and we were forced to return to the hotel, having belatedly remembered that the hotel-keeper had invited us to have a drink with him. However, when we found him he was draped across a chair: bored with waiting for us, he had finished all the ale himself. We had to break into our high-altitude rations, and three bottles of gin rapidly disappeared.

Rondoy

The next morning, all a little hungover, we spent lazing around in the sun. Occasionally the silence was broken with afterthoughts to the main argument of the previous night: namely, the greatness, or otherwise, of Wales, with Charlie Powell answering all disparaging comments about Wales with the same retort: 'You don't know what you're talking about.' Midday saw us on our way to the teachers' fiesta. It turned out to be more like a church garden-party than anything else; and after sampling one or two of the local brews, and listening to some English records played in our honour, we left. It will always remain a puzzle to me how records of such English tunes as 'The Desert Song', 'Tramp, Tramp, Tramp', and 'It's a long way to Tipperary', came to this Andean town, a relic of the Inca Empire.

Crossing the main square we encountered some of our friends of the previous night. Although the Indians themselves are shy of foreigners, the half-breed Peruvians are very friendly and waste no opportunity to try out the little English that they have somehow picked up. Dave Condict found himself greatly embarrassed by one objectionable man who insisted on saying continually and in a loud voice, that he liked Dave. When he discovered that this made the rest of us laugh, he proudly repeated it with even more conviction, thereby increasing our amusement and Dave's embarrassment.

We wandered into the Indian market where, as a contrast to the suavity of the *mestizos* to whom we had just been talking, the Indian stallholders met with fits of giggling all our attempts to purchase items of food and equipment. We gave up, and scoured the shops for things we still required: fruit, bread, cans, paraffin, and petrol. The one thing we had found almost impossible to buy all the way from Lima to Chiquian—refined salt—turned up in enormous quantities in a shop belonging to the hotel-keeper's mother. We also bought some sacks for the trek, and began to make up the loads. Meanwhile, Alvarez had arrived back from Popca with twenty-eight animals. He said that he would come round in the morning at seven o'clock, but asked us for some money for the animals' evening meal. We were a little put out at this, as we had understood that he would be responsible for feeding the *burros*, while we should be responsible for feeding him and his men. Not so, he said; we should have to feed the animals in Chiquian and he would feed them after that. This seemed a little one-sided to us, as once we left Chiquian the animals' food would be free anyway! We paid him 100 *soles* extra. We were beginning to learn that any price quoted is a minimum only.

After dinner most of us went to bed early to be fresh for the long walk ahead of us next day. Charlie had gone off drinking with a friend whom he had made in the hotel—a chap who had told us that he was the local 'Inspector of School Books'. While they were out they met Pete Bebbington, newly arrived, who was wandering round the streets looking for us. Pete and Charlie came on to the hotel, bearing a bottle of foul spirits with which to celebrate, and so we lost our early night. Dave Condict was engaged in his favourite occupation—sleep—when they arrived in our hotel room. They were already tipsy, and Pete Bebbington proceeded to pelt the prostrate Condict with bars of chocolate and packets of nuts. When he awoke under the barrage, Dave did not seem too pleased to see Pete. Pete, had often told us of how, when in the navy, it had been the custom to drink heavily whenever the ship arrived in port; Dave now commented that Pete seemed to be regarding Chiquian as yet another port.

Luckily the muleteers arrived two hours late the next morning. If we had given the matter any thought we should have been prepared for this. Late as it was, we were still in bed when the cry went up that the *burros* had arrived. Down in the hotel yard we found the saddest assortment of animals that I have ever seen: twenty-one *burros* that looked as if it was all they could do to carry their own weight, four defeated looking horses (at least, they were *called* horses), and three defiant, aggressive mules which we were to change for *burros* at Popca.

43

Loading pack-animals is a fine art. Nothing is used except strips of cloth and lengths of rope, the cloth being used to hold the load in place and the rope to bind it tight. The rope is tightened by placing a foot on the wretched animal's flank and tugging hard. We were surprised to find that the muleteers expected us to provide most of the rope. This being a scarce commodity in the Chiquian area, we were forced to cut a 500-foot hemp rope into twenty-foot pieces. Each animal was loaded with about 80 lb and then goaded out into the street. The street was crowded with sightseers, and I was a little sceptical of the safety of the loads; but nothing was lost except a few sheets of plastic wrapping. Eventually we ran out of animals with about three hundredweight of loads still to go. Alvarez arranged for four *burros* to come down to pick them up on Tuesday, July 9th—two days later—when Pete Bebbington would be following us after a short period of acclimatization.

At twelve o'clock noon we set off, a strange assortment of men and beasts winding its lazy way down the dusty street crowded with Indian children yelling 'good-bye, meester'. The feeling that at last we were really on our way to the mountains faded at the outskirts of the town. We had to stop to readjust all the loads, which were slipping; and for an hour or so we sat admiring and photographing the view across the valleys and foothills, above which soared the ridge of the Cordillera Huay huash. We wondered where Graham and Vic would be, for they had set off early in the morning of the previous day to find a good site for base camp.

Eventually we began to move again; Pete Westnidge and Dave Condict took the lead, followed by the *burros* and Indian overseers. Pete Farrell, Charlie, and myself brought up the rear. Presiding over the whole caravan was Alvarez, the *arriero*, aristocratically perched on his horse, his face twisted into a cynical smile. At first we stopped every few minutes to reload some *burro* whose pack had fallen off. The first few miles were downhill and the total effect was that of a rather pleasant ramble. We were all in good humour, the weather was fine and the scenery impressive. We stopped to talk with an occasional farmer (Charlie with their daughters), smoked a cigarette, ate an orange, and rambled on again. The path dropped into the river valley, and as it descended the vegetation became more lush until, walking along the bank of the river, it was almost as if we were in a tropical jungle. The trees rose to form a canopy over our heads, blotting out the sun. The air was still, and full of the sounds of insects and birds, and the roar of the river. After a few miles the track crossed the river and became lost in a sandy flat that was obviously the river's flood-bed in the rainy season. The vegetation was sparser here, and on both sides of us the land rose steeply. We followed the tracks of the *burros* across the sand and soon the path began to climb the steep hillside.

The ramble suddenly became more arduous as altitude and lack of oxygen made each step an unpleasant effort. I began to take quick short breaths and my pulse raced. Added to this discomfort were the blisters on my feet, caused by the new, narrow-fitting French boots which I was trying to break in before starting to climb. Pete Farrell was setting the pace for us three behind the *burros*: fresh from a season in the New Zealand Alps, he seemed to have only one speed, regardless of gradient. Charlie and I began to fall behind him, and eventually I dropped behind Charlie. We were still moving faster than the *burros*; and whenever Pete Farrell caught up with them, he would rest and wait for Charlie and me to appear. The blisters on my feet burst and I was forced to stop and attend to them. Consequently I fell so far behind that it became impossible for me to catch up again. I walked on along the path, slowly gaining height. The hillside rose steeply on one side and fell away for several hundred feet on the other. The sun disappeared, and in the twilight I lost the tracks, taking eventually a wrong turning which led me, after half a mile, into a farmyard. Cursing, I reversed and found the fork. I was not surprised that I had gone astray, as the main path suddenly lost itself on some steps that led directly into a mass of undergrowth. I later learned that Vic had made an arrow out of stones at the junction, which—in the rapidly failing light—I had missed. The path led into a very high-walled ravine, across a precarious bridge, and into trees which grew alongside the raging torrent of a river. I stopped and ate half an orange, the only food I had left. By now the light had gone completely and the night was absolutely black. After stumbling on for some time, using the stars as guides, I gave up the attempt to reach the camp. I was bored with walking into trees and rocks.

With the light from a cigarette-lighter I found a piece of flat rock for my airbed and settled down for the night. I drank an enormous quantity of water to dull the ache in my stomach, and went off to sleep immediately. I slept with my boots on to stop my feet from swelling in the night, cursing the French for having such narrow feet. I woke in the middle of the night to find that the moon was shining directly into the ravine. The moonlight was so bright that it was possible to see the path ahead. I turned over and slept again until the morning.

I was awakened at dawn by the grunting of pigs a few feet from my face, and found a little Indian boy staring at me. He was, he told me, on his way with the pigs to Llamac, where the rest of the *gringos* were encamped. As I walked with him I was surprised to find that I had slept only a few hundred yards from the village, where I found the motley group of *gringos* huddled around stoves, brewing a breakfast of beans, jam, bread, and coffee. They were camped on what seemed to be the village green, and had attracted the usual attention of a horde of children. Charlie was fending them off with shouts and stones as I walked into the camp site.

After breakfast I felt much better; and while Alvarez and his men were rounding up the *burros* and loading them, Charlie and I set off on the next section—up the narrow gorge to Popca. Both Llamac and Popca are built on fairly level ground between ravines along the river. The soil is relatively fertile, producing—as well as rice and the usual potatoes (the potato plant originated in Peru)—small yields of other crops such as maize and sugar. In fields close to the village small herds of healthy-looking cattle were grazing, and huge black pigs scoured around everywhere. Along the paths we saw several herds of goats. Between Llamac and Popca the river gorge was well cultivated, and trees and tall grasses grew in profusion. Colourful butterflies and tiny humming-birds abounded. The whole effect was that of a thriving community and contributed to a pleasant walk in the morning sun.

Popca is a much more primitive village than Llamac. Whereas in Llamac it was not unusual to find houses reasonably well constructed with odd pieces of corrugated iron or slabs of concrete, the houses in Popca were built entirely of mud-brick with earth roofs. In Llamac the streets had an occasional stretch of paving, and there was even a swimming pool; the streets in Popca were of dust-covered earth or of mud where the open drains ran. All the houses off the main square were built on earth foundations and had steps cut out of the earth up to the doors, which were mainly on the first floor. At many of the doors old and wizened women sat spinning wool. Charlie and I made for the shop, where we bought some beer; and we then sat in the main square, waiting for the others.

The first loaded *burro* soon appeared, closely followed by the others, until eventually the whole square seemed to be full of braying animals trying to escape down the side alleys. We halted here for a while for the loads to be taken off the three mules and switched to the three *burros* that had been waiting to replace them. While we waited, the five of us sat on a bench in the middle of the square. We sat drinking beer amidst the confusion of animals and children, taking photographs and watching with amusement an old man railing at Alvarez. Alvarez had evidently hired some of the *burros* from him, and he was now objecting both to the way they were loaded and to the weight of their loads. We gave him some beer and he quietened down.

Rondoy

No sooner had we set off, after an hour or so's rest, than we ran into trouble trying to keep the *burros* on the right track. Most of them came from farms around Popca and they began to scatter here and there in search of their home comforts. With shouts, thwacks, and prods, the muleteers brought them back onto the path into the next ravine, which was steep and rocky. The ravine led into a long, deep, V-shaped gorge, the path gaining height all the way, which ran along one side. The vegetation here tended more towards flowering shrubs and bushes, and the path was dry and dusty. Gradually the *burros*, keeping their steady pace, began to overtake us, sending up clouds of dust to add to the discomforts caused by the altitude. We finally arrived at the top of the gorge where the path led into a small settlement of pastoral farmers, whose children encouraged us with yells of '*gringo*'. The path through the huts led onto the *Pampa de los Toros*—the Plain of Bulls. We made a good speed across this flat stretch, but failed to catch up with the *burros*. At the far end of the two-mile-square plain the hills closed in again and the path led into another long, but less steep gorge, at the top of which I began to feel very tired. Suddenly looking up I saw the fierce west face of Rondoy, towering above. The psychological effect of seeing Rondoy so close was stimulating, though short-lived. Needing a rest, Dave Condict and I stopped beside a river, where I slept for a short time, while Dave pulled out his toilet-bag and proceeded to wash off the day's accumulated dust. I was sleeping in the shade of a bridge made out of tree trunks, and was awakened by a herd of domesticated llamas clattering across it. It is unusual to see llamas in this part of Peru. They are mainly found on the *Altiplano* in the south, and these were the first that either of us had seen.

We set off soon after, a little refreshed; but after half a mile or so uphill we began to feel exhausted again and sat down for a rest. Dave, discovering that he had left his sun-glasses at the bridge, turned round with some blood-curdling curses and went back for them, while I sat and waited for him. When he returned, we were a little worried about the route, for the others were now so far ahead that we could not see them. We guessed that they would be at the far end of the plain onto which our path was leading us. We could not be sure, however, for we knew that we must be close to the path leading up to the first of two passes across the Huayhuash ridge—the Kasha Punta—which Vic and Graham were assumed to have crossed on the way in. We plodded on until I noticed several horses in a paddock, and suggested to Dave Condict that we should try to hire a couple of them from the farm. We thought that we still had to cross the Andes that day, for it was only two o'clock in the afternoon. He said he would rather walk, to get fit, but would give me his pack if I managed to hire a horse. So he ambled on while I walked across to the farmer's hut.

It took a long time for me to communicate my needs to the farmer, for both of us spoke little Spanish, our only common language. His first language was Quechua, the ancient Inca tongue. It turned out later that he was trying to tell me that it was not worth the trouble of bringing a horse down from their paddock, as the main party was only about half a mile away, camped out of sight over the lip of a slope. He failed to get this across to me, however, and several minutes later I was mounted, bareback, on a white horse, with the Indian farmer running in front.

We soon caught up with Dave Condict, and I took his pack. This turned out to be an almost useless gesture, for one minute later, as we went over the top of the slope, we saw that the others were camped fifty yards away. Pete Farrell, Charlie, and Pete Westnidge were propped up against the walls of a hut that they had made out of the *burro*-loads. Though the horse had turned out to be useless for transport purposes, it was worth the money for the amusement provided by their faces as I rode in on my white 'charger'.

The camp site was at the foot of the Kakanan Pass which we were to cross the following morning. We put up the tent on a little plain at the end of a hanging valley; the plain was probably a filled-in glacial lake, and its sole tenant was an Indian farmer who, with his family, kept a few cows and pigs. After the sun had set we had our first experience of the sudden change in temperature that marks the end of the day in the high Andes. The five of us crowded into the shelter built for the Indians to sleep in, and set-to preparing the evening stew. The Indians clustered round outside in their *ponchos*. Nobody felt much like sitting up after the meal, so, leaving the Indians to move into their shelter, we settled down for the night. Dave Condict, Pete Westnidge, and I slept in the tent, Pete Farrell and Charlie electing to sleep out.

In the morning we found the inside walls of the tent covered with ice. Charlie had slept with his head outside his sleeping-bag and woke to find his hair frozen. It looked as though it would be a long time before we started, as the *burros* were evidently not keen to continue, and each one had to be caught before it could be loaded. As it was none too pleasant standing in the cold, Pete Westnidge, Charlie, and I set off up the side of a shoulder that sloped down from the ridge to the valley below us. It was quite steep, but the going was made easier by the path, which was broken into a series of short zig-zags. These were essential if the pass was to be used by loaded pack-animals. The path was precarious in places, leading across steep scree slopes and including an occasional rock-pitch. It was hard to believe that the *burros* would be able to negotiate some of the harder sections. We were in the cold shadow of the mountain and it was some consolation to see that the ridge we were heading for was in the sunshine.

We rested for a short while at the top of the pass, which we estimated at 15,500 feet, and took off some of our now surplus clothing. It was good to be in the sunlight again—at least, it was at first, when we were grateful for the warmth. Another lure towards reaching the top of the ridge proved to be disappointing. We had expected spectacular views, but what we found was a view across seemingly endless rows of rolling hills and empty

15. 'Prince Philip' in the foreground, with Jirishanca Chico
to left and Jirishanca Grande to right, with Yerupaja Chico
between them in the distance

16. Looking beyond Jirishanca Chico towards the Amazon
Basin at dawn

valleys. The Huayhuash is the watershed of South America, and although—away in the distance—we could see clouds forming in the Amazon Basin, there was not much to be seen of the mountains which we were heading for.

From the pass the path zig-zagged down a very steep shoulder. At about 14,500 feet it levelled out and seemed to disappear. Away to the south-east I saw Pete Westnidge on the crest of a hill. I shouted to him but could not make out his reply, so decided to take a route that would bring me to the same point. The muleteers followed us, assuming that we knew where we wanted to go. It was too brave an assumption, for our route involved a great deal of unnecessary effort. We discovered later that if we had found the path it would have taken us to base camp by a much easier route.

The route we had chosen, out of ignorance, led across a series of high drumlins (glacial hills) covered with dust and tufts of needle-sharp *puna* grass. Once we were over the first ridge, the peaks of Rondoy and Jirashanca came into view, with their slopes and glaciers. It was quite hard going across these hills, and once again we straggled out. After three or four miles I saw the main party in the distance, apparently setting up the base camp. It seemed an unpromising spot, close to nothing in particular and without running water. As I approached I heard the sounds of an argument. Reaching the group I found all the *burros* unloaded, the Indians and Alvarez infuriated, and Westnidge, Condict, and Farrell exasperated. It seemed that Pete Farrell had signalled to the men with the *burros* to halt, while he went ahead to see if he could see Vic and Graham. Alvarez had mistaken the signal to mean unload, and, as no one else was there to contradict, he had unloaded. By the time the next person arrived, the *burros* were completely unladen, straggling all over the hills, and the men were waiting to be paid. When Pete Farrell arrived back, having seen Graham and the base camp site, he furiously tried to make Alvarez and his men reload the animals. But Alvarez was not interested: he wanted payment, pointing out that if he did not start back at once he would not be able to recross the pass before nightfall.

I arrived in the middle of this chaos. With a splitting *sorroche* headache, I was none too willing to join in the argument. But Pete Farrell stormed off in his exasperation, leaving me as the only Spanish speaker, and a poor one at that. The headache solved the problem for me, for I was not to be dragged into the argument at any price. I simply issued an ultimatum: Alvarez wanted his money and we would not pay him until the loads were in base camp. We agreed that the situation was the result of a misunderstanding and offered to add a few hundred *soles* to the price and also to feed the men for the night. As he was still unmoved I promised that we would send for him when the time came to leave the mountains. This tipped the balance: grudgingly they reloaded, while we set about rounding up the outlying *burros*.

Ahead of us the route lay across a plateau and went down a steep slope to the bank of a lake. Then it followed the bank for a while before rising slightly to a small area of level ground between two lakes, where we could see one or two figures moving. On the way down the slope one of the insecure loads fell off and a large can of dried milk fell a few hundred feet, though without opening. Charlie took the opportunity of pointing out that it was from a Welsh dairy. Soon we were unloading for the second time and stacking the stores. Four of us put up the tents while the other three prepared the evening meal. Once again people were more eager to sleep than to sit about chatting, and soon after supper we all went off to our tents. The muleteers were sleeping in the tent destined for our stores. They intended to be up and away before dawn the following morning, but we ourselves had no desire to rise early.

The sun was well up the next morning when the first of us, Vic as usual, crept out of his tent. The Indians, complete with *burros*, had already disappeared. The night had not brought much rest for some of us, because of the effect of the altitude. I myself had lain awake most of the night with aching throat, bleeding gums, and sunburn. Most of us at some time during the expedition suffered from what Pete Farrell told us was called Cheyne-Stokes breathing. It only occurs during sleep, and results from the body giving up its attempt to gain enough oxygen from the thin air. If it happens to yourself, it is not so bad, as it wakes you up and you quickly gasp for breath in rapid pants. It is worse when, as you are lying awake, someone else suddenly stops breathing. You lie there with nerves tense, wondering who it is and hoping it is really only a temporary stop. Suddenly, whoever it is gasps, choking with the rush of air, and you can relax again. That first night I woke up several times gasping for breath. It was quite a relief to be up and about in the warm sun.

After breakfast we set about organizing the camp, making two separate piles of gear, one of food and one of climbing equipment. The effort was wasted, for when Pete Bebbington arrived two days later we rearranged the whole camp. But the preliminary sorting out revealed that by some drastic oversight the cigarettes had been left behind in Chiquian, with the stores Pete Bebbington was bringing up. The most important job was to set up the dart-board, which took three of us the best part of the day. The food was sorted into two separate piles: high-altitude rations and base camp stores. The only significance that this distinction came to have was, that when we used high-altitude rations in base camp— which we often did—Food Officer Charlie Powell would throw his arms up in disgust. This came to be one of the delights of high-altitude rations.

By noon the flies had found us. The last thing in the world we could possibly have expected to find at a base camp 14,500 feet up in the Andes, was man-eating flies. The fact that they were so slow that they could be squashed while actually biting, gave us no consolation, for their number was inexhaustible. Their presence was later explained to us by the local farmer. He told us that we were camped above a piece of marshy land that was the traditional 'burial ground' where animals came to die, and where the flies bred and battened on their carcases.

The camp was sited more or less at the focus of a semi-circle ridge that included Ninashanca, Rondoy, Jirishanca, and Jirishanca Chico. The ridge ranged in height from approximately 16,200 feet (Jirishanca Chico) to a little over 20,000 on Jirishanca. Below them lay the huge Egger and Oggioni glaciers. Soon we became used to the roars of avalanches at all times of the day and night, as pieces of these glaciers broke away and crashed down hundreds of feet into Ninakocha, the lake directly below them.

Ninakocha was dammed in by a huge terminal moraine and it was below this that we were camped. A stream of glacial melt water ran past the site, about thirty yards away. Even this short walking distance was enough to tire one at this height. We allocated stretches of the stream for body washing, clothes washing, crockery washing, and an automatically flushing W.C. The water was so cold that to have a complete bath was a test of stamina, and you had to feel very dirty indeed before you risked it. A few yards further down, the stream cascaded over a steep *roche moutonnée* onto the 'burial ground' below. Charlie suggested this cascade as a shower-bath; he was its only victim, and that only for a few brief seconds!

The 'burial ground' was about a quarter-mile square of semi-bog land bordering the larger lake Mitukocha. I suspected that the lake had once been higher but had at some time broken through the wall of moraine that had dammed it in, leaving an area of peaty bog at both ends. Beyond the lake was an area of several square miles of pasture, grazed by a surprisingly magnificent herd of cattle. We later discovered that the stretch of a river named Rio Machaycancha, running through this, was filled with enormous trout. Further still, the valley changed to a more or less easterly direction carrying the river down to the Marañón.

The setting was perfect. Sitting in the brilliant sunshine that first afternoon in base camp, we went over our plans. Gazing up from time to time we could actually see the mountains we were talking about, and were not just looking at their names on a map in London. We planned to concentrate all our efforts at first on Rondoy, partly as an insurance against it being more difficult than we expected, and partly to leave ourselves as much time as possible for the other peaks we hoped to scale.

From where we sat we could see two peaks of Rondoy; the rock peak of Rondoy Chico, then an ice-cone summit behind it and higher. This ice summit turned out later to be Rondoy North, though at that time we were not quite sure. As the only photographs we had were taken from other aspects, it was difficult to make out whether this peak was the summit peak. It was certainly the highest point on Rondoy that we could see; but we discovered later that the south (and higher) summit was visible only from the north summit. The north summit had already been climbed by Walter Bonatti, and we now tried to work out which of the two possible approaches he had used. The ridges of Rondoy took the shape of a Y. The stem was a ridge leading from the ice-cone to the peak of Rondoy Chico; the junction between the arms and stem was the ice-cone; the right-hand arm led to Ninashanca and formed a basin; the other arm enclosed another ice-basin as it led up to Jirishanca.

The left-hand (as we faced it) ice-basin was hidden from our view. Out of the other ice-basin, which we could see into, rose a snow-and-ice-face leading up to the ridge. This was the north-west face which we calculated Bonatti had used for access to the ridge, and which was the one that the Peruvian authorities had allocated to us for our attempt. The south-east face had been allocated to the American expedition.

Our first problem was to find a route into the ice-basin. A lateral moraine led from the base camp to the tip of the tongue of the glacier that hung over the lip of the basin. From there we proposed to try to find a route through the ice-fall up into the basin. Once in the basin, the route up to the ridge would have to be worked out again, but it looked as though the ice-face would be the most promising feature of the high and steep wall which almost encircled the basin.

After supper, which was the 'sort-of-stew' that was to be our staple diet at base camp, we prepared loads of approximately 30 lb. These contained the equipment and food necessary to establish a camp in the ice-basin. Six of us were to set off the following morning at five o'clock, leaving Dave Condict behind in base camp.

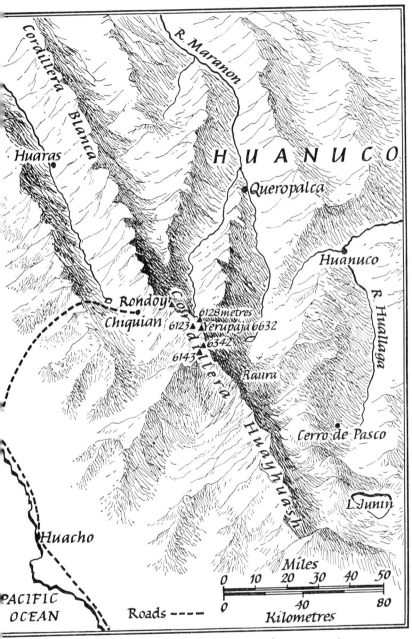

Detail map showing Chiquian and the surrounding mountain ranges

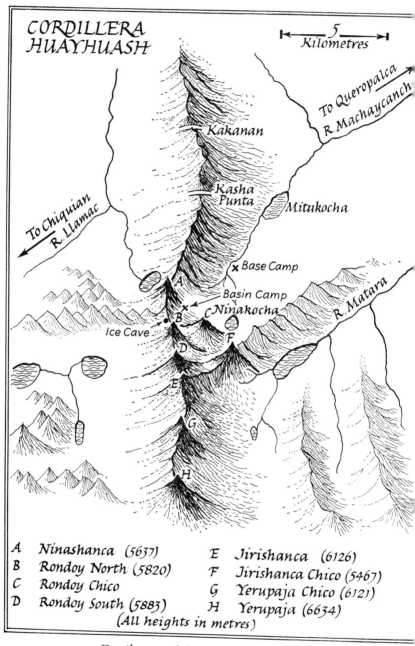

CORDILLERA
HUAYHUASH

5
Kilometres

To Queropalca
R. Machaycanch

Kakanan

Kasha
Punta

Mitukocha

To Chiquian
R. Llamac

× Base Camp

A

Basin Camp
× C. Ninakocha

Ice Cave

B

F

D

R. Matara

E

G

H

A	Ninashanca (5637)	E	Jirishanca (6126)
B	Rondoy North (5820)	F	Jirishanca Chico (5467)
C	Rondoy Chico	G	Yerupaja Chico (6121)
D	Rondoy South (5883)	H	Yerupaja (6634)

(All heights in metres)

Detail map of the Cordillera Huayhuash

17. The first abseil on the route into the ice-basin

19. Route map

20. At the top of the first abseil

21. On the triangular flake which blocked the traverse ledge

4

The Ice-Basin

The next day, July 12th, began for me at 4 a.m. with Vic shaking my shoulders. We were short of tents until Pete Bebbington arrived; and as I was sleeping in the kitchen tent, nothing could be done while I was still in my sleeping-bag. I struggled into my breeches and string vest, and helped Vic with the breakfast. In half an hour we were all up, except Dave Condict; and it wasn't until we were struggling up the first steep slopes that we appreciated that he was staying in base camp because he had *lost* at dice the night before.

Soon after five we set off in the gloom of dawn. The lateral moraine leading up to the glacier started almost at the camp site, and a few minutes after leaving the camp we were all breathing quickly. For a long while the only thought in my head was how to breath most efficiently. Anything that disturbed the rhythm caused me to gasp rapidly, since the body needed more oxygen to meet any extra demand for energy. Coughing, sneezing, or stumbling on the loose rocks, for example, were followed by rapid, almost frantic breathing. I seemed to be having the most trouble, judging by the noise, though everybody was to some extent distressed. At first we stopped quite frequently to check the route ahead, and the stops were very much appreciated. The path lay up the crest of the moraine, which fell away steeply: on one side into the glacial lake Ninakocha, and on the other into a small valley which carried the stream of melt-water from the glacier we were heading for.

Ninakocha was an impressive lake. Of pure crystal blue, it was overhung with glaciers, from which great blocks of ice would occasionally snap, hurtling into the lake below to form miniature icebergs which the sun gradually melted. From the great glacier below Jirishanca hung a huge waterfall of ice, feeding directly into the lake and with its lowest reaches submerged.

There was little time or inclination now, however, to admire the view; and after a short rest at the top of the moraine we went on up a series of short rock-walls with steep grass terraces between. Traversing round the tongue of the glacier we scrambled up to the base of Rondoy Chico. Here we roped up, put on our crampons and snow-goggles, and with the help of ice-axes ventured onto the ice-fall. At first we made good speed across small snow-covered ice terraces, gaining height by means of connecting ice-ramps. Eventually the only way we could make any progress through the séracs was by climbing up vertical walls of ice. Every time we went over a wall we came up against another. In many places the walls were overhanging, and the ice had rotted through into fantastic patterns. The condition of the ice, combined with the continuous creaks and groans coming from the many crevasses, did little to reassure us of the safety of the route. In the end, Pete Farrell, who was leading, turned round, shrugged his shoulders and said one word: 'suicidal'. Nobody disagreed.

Vic and I having been the last rope on the way up, were now in front, and we took advantage of being a fair way ahead to explore another route. We met with the same conditions and once again retreated. When we had rejoined the others, we all sat at the base of Rondoy Chico, perched on the top of the moraine left by the glacier at its exit from the ice-basin. As we ate the food we had brought with us for the day we talked over the morning's climbing. It was obvious that the ice-fall was not going to provide us with a route into the basin. The only alternative was to climb some way up the walls of either Rondoy Chico or Ninas-hanca and try to drop down into the basin from above. To test this theory Pete Farrell and Vic set off up the wall of Rondoy Chico that loomed directly behind and above us. The rest of us dumped our loads, to save carrying them up again when the breakthrough was eventually made.

Soon after we arrived back at base camp, Pete Bebbington was seen on the sky-line, complete with four *burros*. I noted in my diary for the day that Pete's efficiency, drive, and leadership soon became evident. In the two hours before darkness he rearranged the whole camp site. Somewhere we had lost two sets of tent-poles; Pete got over this loss by stretching a 300-foot rope across two rocks on either side of the camp, and hanging the tents from it. The line was kept tight by means of two pieces of Dexion balanced on top of two cartons of tinned food. The line inevitably came to be used as a clothes line and for airing sleeping-bags; the Dexion served as dartboard support, radio-aerial, and flag-pole.

In the twilight we heard shouts and, looking up, saw Pete Farrell and Vic making their way down the moraine. They had gained sufficient height on Rondoy Chico to confirm the impossibility of making a route through the ice-fall into the basin.

That evening, over supper, we described the day's climbing to Pete Bebbington and explained why we thought it impossible to make a route through the ice-fall. The general feeling at the time was, as Pete Farrell put it, that Rondoy was going to prove a 'toughy'. We planned, after a day's rest, to split up into three parties which would take three different routes and work out the possibilities. Pete Bebbington and Graham were to try the route via Ninashanca; Pete Farrell and Vic were to try to get a good view of the basin by climbing to the top of Rondoy Chico; while Charlie, Pete Westnidge and Dave Condict were to aim at working out a possible traverse from Rondoy Chico into the ice-basin. Then, tired after the day's climbing, we went early again to bed. As we settled down we could hear the thunderclaps of a storm far away in the Amazon basin.

The *mestizo* who had come with Pete Bebbington wanted to be off early the next morning. As I was still sleeping in the kitchen tent, I was roused at six by Pete Bebbington who had come across to make the muleteer's breakfast. I had not had a good night and was pleased to have someone to talk to. Like most of us, I had been badly sunburnt the day before, and it was this that kept me awake. Throughout the night I could hear coughing coming from Pete Westnidge who had caught a bad cold and had also slept little.

After the *burros* left, it began to snow heavily. Graham heard the stoves going and came across to join us. We sat round the stoves talking for a couple of hours while the storm worsened, the warmth of the morning eventually turning the snow to rain. Near midday the rain stopped, the clouds parted and the sun came out, and with the sun, the flies.

We lunched on 'high-altitude herrings' and 'high-altitude vegetable salad', after which Graham and I walked down to try our luck fishing in Mitukocha. As the lake was very much silted at the edges, it was difficult with our tackle—a length of nylon and a butterfly hook—to reach the deeper water in the centre. It meant that one of us had to hold the end of the line while the other walked away along the bank until the line was fully extended, and then throw the hook as far as possible towards the centre. We walked the complete circumference of the lake doing this, taking two and a half hours. Graham was always inclined to be quiet in a group, but enjoyed talking when alone with someone. He told me his plans for the future, showing that—unlike the rest of us— he knew what he wanted out of life. This, he said, was to be his last serious climbing expedition, as he thought it inconsiderate to inflict so much anxiety on one's family and close friends: and though climbing was an important part of his life, it was not everything. You only learned to know Graham when you got him to yourself like this. In general, he was so quiet and withdrawn that you hardly noticed he was there.

The only result of our afternoon's fishing was a very bloated pig. While we were talking we saw three Indians making for the camp. We discovered later that they had traded a sack of potatoes and some cheese, for biscuits and empty tins. So far from civilization, empty tins of any sort were scarce and valuable, and after this we often had visitors asking for tins and cartons.

After supper, we talked late into the night; all except Charlie who had begun to plough his way through the expedition's favourite book, *War and Peace*. The conversation centred round Rondoy—there was little else we could think about. Pete Farrell kept us laughing with tales about climbing in the New Zealand Alps. Even our expedition's 'dark horse', Vic, enjoyed recounting tales of climbing in New Zealand: tales of flat-mates who kept fit by bending thick steel rods; of visiting Limey climbers being beaten up in fish-and-chip shops; and of the women members who had finally tamed the wilder elements of the Canterbury Climbing Club. Some of Pete Farrell's stories were news to Vic, who had been away from New Zealand for eighteen months. While we were talking, Pete Farrell took off his cap for a moment —the first time we had seen him with it off. He looked ten years younger. With his cap on, and his broad Manchester accent, Pete is something of a cross between Don Whillans and a dapper Ted Ray, with characteristic phrases to match both characters; sharing with the Whillans 'awa the noo', with Ted Ray 'by jove, yes!' besides having many phrases of his own, the most typical being 'me old tater'. Both Pete Farrell and Vic have a marked sense of humour; but while they kept us laughing in base camp, on the mountains they are quiet and determined, and throughout the expedition they inspired confidence in the rest of us.

It was after midnight when, largely out of discomfort from sitting on biscuit-tins for several hours, we stretched our legs before settling down for the night. The moonlight was brilliant, and the peaks of Rondoy—silvered against the night sky—thrust impressively through a layer of cloud.

We were a little worried about the amount of cloud that had been building up each afternoon over the previous few days, and especially after the storm of that morning. Normally, July and

Rondoy

August are completely cloudless months in the Peruvian Andes, for the rains do not usually start until the middle of September; it looked as though we might be in for some meteorological bad luck.

Next morning the weather was no better, and it was eleven o'clock before it was clear enough for anyone to set off on the day's climbing programme. Pete Farrell and Vic, Dave Condict, Pete Westnidge, and Charlie set off together up the moraine, while Pete Bebbington and Graham went off in the opposite direction.

Pete and Graham were the first back in base camp in the afternoon, where I had hot drinks ready in vacuum flasks. They had drawn a blank in their attempt to find a route into the basin from the Ninashanca side. What they did find, however, was an excellent site for a camp from which to make an attempt on the summit of Ninashanca. Not long after, Charlie, Pete Westnidge, and Dave Condict returned. They had even better news. They had followed Vic and Pete Farrell's route up the lower slopes of Rondoy Chico to the top of a huge triangular pinnacle of rock. From this vantage point, they had seen a possible route down a gully, traversing round to the basin. They decided not to go down the gully and so risk a bivouac that night, and had instead retraced their steps to base camp.

Pete Farrell and Vic had left Charlie, Dave, and Pete on the lower slopes and bivouacked that night on the ridge of Rondoy Chico. In the afternoon we had watched their progress until it was obvious that they were going to have to spend the night up there. We saw them cross a snowfield in the twilight, then—switching on their head-lamps—continue down a little further before stopping and settling for the night.

This is what they told us later. When they had arrived at the food and fuel dump we had taken up a few days earlier, they had repacked their day-sacks. Though neither spoke, they both knew their own and each other's intentions for the day from the types

64

of sacks they were using and the items they were packing in them. At first they moved independently, initially up steep grass gullies and then across scree slopes to a 100-foot wall of rock. The wall was negotiated by means of a series of chimneys, each of about 'just severe' standard. Above the wall they gained height on rock terraces, broken by small rock steps of ten to fifteen feet in height, the impression being that of a giant staircase. Coming across a small snowfield they roped up; then, cutting steps alternately, they quickly gained another 400 feet. This brought them onto the ridge. From here they had a good view into the basin, and they sat for a while looking for a means of access. Not being encouraged by what they saw, they went on up the ridge.

The summit (of Rondoy Chico) gave the impression, as summits always do, of being quite close above them. Soon they admitted to each other what they had already suspected: that they were going to have to spend the night out. Climbing up the last ridge, of hard snow, the easing-off of the angle gave the illusion of a summit. It turned out to be a false summit. The real summit was still three or four rope-lengths away. As it was now quite late they decided to look for a bivouac site before it was too dark, and started to descend. A little below the snow-slope they found a small ledge, with enough room for one of them to sleep in a sitting position, and the other half-crouching. There was a light cloud round them for most of the night, which only cleared occasionally. At one in the morning it began to snow. Vic managed to sleep for three or four hours, waking up to find a cover of snow over him, frozen into a shell. Nevertheless, he had a comfortable night, being tolerably warm. They made a brew of tea at about four o'clock, and slowly prepared to leave the ledge as soon as it was light. With the dawn came an incredibly clear, crisp morning; and as they picked their way down the mountain, neither felt fatigued after their night out.

They arrived back at base camp soon after noon, to find the rest of us making up packs with which to establish a camp on

Ninashanca. We set off in blazing sunshine, with only the mere suspicion of a cloud on the horizon. The first stretch was up a very steep grass slope opposite the camp; it was hard, hot going and we zig-zagged up the contours to make it a little easier. Over the top of this slope we came to the plateau where we had had the altercation with the *burro*-men over reloading. This plateau was abruptly bordered on one side by a wall of rock sixty or seventy feet high. The few gullies that broke the wall seemed too difficult to climb with packs, so we wandered along the route by which we had come in with the *burros*. At the beginning of the drumlins we found a grass-covered shoulder leading up to the top of the first rock-wall. In the hour it took us to reach this point, those few wisps of cloud we had seen on the horizon had been rapidly building up, until now the whole sky was overcast. And with the disappearance of the sun it became quite cold: most of us stopped to put on sweaters and anoraks. We encountered some grazing cattle which Charlie Powell scattered with his 'Glamorgan cattle cry'.

At the point where the shoulder reached the top of the rock-wall we were surprised to find a fence with a gate and stile. We were later told by the farmer of this land that he rented out the pastures, such as they were, above this gate and fence, and grazed his own cattle in the much better pastures below it. We doubled back towards base camp, along the top of the cliff, gaining height all the time, until we reached a succession of rock-ledges and scree slopes, which we zig-zagged up. A wind had built up by now and it was bitter cold. Reaching some small snowfields, we kicked steps up to the spot which Pete Bebbington and Graham had found the day before. It was situated on the top of one of the snowfields, where it levelled off, providing a platform about fifteen feet square. It was in a fairly sheltered spot, more or less directly above base camp, and lay at the foot of a glacier below the great snowcones which, one on top of another, covered Ninashanca, forming its summit. We unloaded our packs there and, leaving Graham

22. Fixed ropes on the last section of the traverse into the ice-basin

23. Pulley system for carrying packs across the crevasses into
the ice-basin

and Charlie behind, started back to base camp. Graham and Charlie were to make the first attempt on Ninashanca the next morning.

Pete Bebbington, Pete Westnidge, and Dave Condict were planning to go next day down the valley to climb Cerro de Paria, a rock peak of close on 17,000 feet. When they looked out of their tents the next morning at seven, they found a thick bank of cloud down to 100 feet or so above the camp. Sighing with relief, the three of them turned over in their sleeping-bags and slept until, at ten-thirty, the sun broke through and began to warm their tents. They resigned themselves to a day's climbing, and went without much gear or food, not expecting to be out very long. They took the same route as the day before, slogging up the grass slope, along the plateau and through the first of the little hills. More slogging up grass slopes brought them to the foot of a snow-gully which led onto the north-east ridge. They climbed solo as much as possible to make good speed. Climbing through broken, messy rock on the ridge, they were eventually faced with the choice of either traversing across a steep gully of loose snow and rotten rock, or breaking out left over a small cornice onto the summit snowfield. They took the latter choice.

As they had not been expecting much snow and ice, they had no crampons, and only one ice-axe, one North-Waller, and one piton hammer between them. They made their way gingerly across the cornice and onto the snowfield, where they found strategically placed rocks which provided good belay positions. From one of these rocks they took it in turn to go up the last pitch to the summit.

One pleasant feature of climbing in a range such as the Huay-huash is that an ascent, even if not a 'first ascent' will probably be a first 'British' ascent. Cerro de Paria had been climbed before both by the Schneider German expedition of 1936, and the Bonatti Italian expedition of 1961. This was the first British ascent. From the top they had a magnificent view, but with little time to enjoy it, for it was already three o'clock in the afternoon. This meant that they would have to make good time on the descent if they were not to be caught by the dark. While near the top they were circled by some of the condors that we had seen flying over the valley. The condor is a really huge bird with a wing-span of some fifteen feet and a body the size of an average pig. It has white-backed wings and trailing legs. It gains height with surprising speed, by using the air currents and seemingly without ever flapping its wings. If disturbed they can be dangerous birds, but normally their only interest in passing humans is one of curiosity. We later learned that at about this time, Lief Patterson's American expedition, a few miles away on the other side of the dividing ridge, was attacked by seven condors while climbing Peak Mexico.

Having thus achieved their objective, Pete Bebbington, Dave Condict, and Pete Westnidge descended Cerro de Paria in two hours, making their way directly down the face. The last section of their descent was a slope of hard snow on which Dave gave an exhibition of glissading, to the amusement of the other two. Arriving back in base camp just before dark, they were surprised to find Charlie there.

Soon after the three of them had left that morning Charlie had returned to base camp on his own. He told us that the previous evening, when Graham and he had been left at the camp site on Ninashanca, they had discovered that they had inadvertently carried up only one stove—an old petrol-stove at that. They coaxed this into giving some heat to cook by, but it was so inefficient that it took a long time to cook anything, and kept giving off great clouds of fumes. They chose to suffer the fumes, rather than open the entrance of the tent to the cold air for ventilation. They had the same problem early the next morning before setting off at dawn.

For them it was a bright, clear morning. The cloud surrounding us at the base camp was inversion cloud, caused by the mixing of air streams of different temperature. By this process, cold air fed into the valley down the hillsides, and mixed with the relatively warm air in the valley, forming a layer of cloud in the bottom of the valley. From above, such cloud looks as if it has been poured into the valley, as a liquid from a jug into a bowl. Thus, while we were completely covered by what appeared from below to be an immense cloud-bank, Charlie and Graham, only a few hundred feet above us, were taking photographs of a glorious dawn.

When they left the tent they climbed up the snowfield on which they had camped until they came onto the ridge, moving all the time at the foot of a large slope of rotten rock. On the ridge they reached the first and lowest of the snow-cones. The snow was soft and Charlie found it hard going. As he was also beginning to feel the effects of the petrol fumes he decided to turn back. They returned to the tent, whence Charlie—leaving Graham there—came down to base camp. He arrived a little after the other three had left for Cerro de Paria, and found Pete Farrell, Vic, and myself lying in the sun, talking. He told us that he had promised Graham that he would send someone up as soon as he arrived. So later in the afternoon Pete Farrell left the camp to join Graham and attempt Ninashanca with him the next day.

Our second visitor came to tea in the afternoon, riding a typical example of the Andean approximation to a horse. He told us that he was the cousin of the local farmer and that he kept the shop in the nearest village. Asked about the bad spell of weather, he said that he thought it would last at least another week—which cheered us greatly! In exchange for some empty tins, he let Vic and me take photos of each other sitting on his trusty nag. After he had gone Vic and I started work on the evening meal, Vic producing a bucketful of unbelievably thick custard that was to keep us chewing for a week.

Pete Bebbington decided that the next day Vic and he would go up to the camp on Ninashanca to make the third attempt, in case Graham and Pete Farrell did not succeed.

Rondoy

The next day brought a change in the weather, for the sun dispersed the night clouds quite early in the morning. After breakfast we played the Huayhuash variation of cricket, with a pack-frame for wickets and an ice-axe as bat. At first it proved so difficult even to hit the ball, that a run was scored every time one managed to do so. Using an ice-axe as a cricket bat is a tricky business, for a false stroke is liable to lodge the 'bat' in the batsman's ankle bone. It remained an open controversy as to which end of the axe was the handle, and which the base. After we had our eye in, we revised the rule about runs, so that they really had to be run for. At 14,500 feet this was no mean achievement, and when gasping for breath after three or four runs, one was glad to hear the ball hit the pack-frame. After two or three innings nobody felt fit enough to continue, so we turned the river into a laundry, bubbling and frothing with best English detergent. Pete Bebbington even went so far as to take a bath in the freezing water. Hearing his yells as he submerged, nobody else felt inclined to join him.

Pete Bebbington and Vic left the base camp at half-past-three in the afternoon, and met Graham and Pete Farrell soon after, on the grass ridge opposite the camp. They had been up to within a couple of hundred feet of the summit, having taken a different route from that of Graham and Charlie the day before. The new route led at first up a gangway of hard snow which, bypassing the soft snow, was quite steep, and led onto the rib at a higher point. Moving higher they crossed a section of loose, rotten rock which gave access to the steep soft snow of the domes directly below the summit. Climbing higher, onto the highest dome, they found a crevasse separating them from the ridge leading to the summit. Pete Farrell negotiated the crevasse but turned back almost immediately, the ridge ice looking too broken and dangerous to support them. They retraced their steps back to the tent and continued down to base camp. Meeting Pete Bebbington and Vic, they passed on all useful information about the route.

Pete and Vic reached the high camp at nightfall. They found

the tent in a squalid condition after the previous tenancies and set
about rehabilitating it. This brought all the tent-pegs out of the
ice, as the sun had loosened them. The ice under the floor of the
tent had melted away for eight inches, and the tent-poles—leaning
inward towards each other—gave a general impression of drunken-
ness. Vic was using the sleeping-bag that Charlie had left in the
tent. Charlie had assured Vic that the bag was adequate. Vic's
comment the next day was that the bag gave as much protection
and warmth as could be expected of a damp tea-towel, and for
once he was happy to get up early. Pete also was in good spirits.

Starting early they made good speed, following the tracks left
by Graham and Pete Farrell up to the point where they had
turned back. This proved to be at the top of the first of four domes;
and where each of these domes gave way to the next, was a
crevasse. Hanging from the upper lips of these crevasses were cur-
tains of gigantic icicles. With one of them belaying in amongst
these icicles, the other would move behind them and cut steps up
onto the upper lip. Then, he in turn would bring up the one who
was belaying. In this way they climbed three of the bulges, until
at the top one they were forced, by the lateness of the afternoon,
to turn back. They arrived in base camp close on nightfall.

While they had been crossing one of the bulges we in base
camp had been able to follow their progress as they took alternate
leads cutting steps, their ice-axes glinting in the sun. In the middle
of the afternoon we had a visit from our landlord. His approach
was announced by loud cracks of his impressive bull-whip. He
was an enormous man of some six and a half feet, accentuated by
a metal sun helmet which, he told us, he had bought in a Lima
junk shop. We never saw him without this helmet. He also wore a
black leather jerkin over a woollen jumper. He told us his name:
Marcial Silva Gastellaños. He was a pleasant character, with his
huge piercing brown eyes, that were at the same time disarmingly
soft. We began to look forward to his visits. He had been born
and educated in Lima. After running a shop in one of the near-by

provincial towns, he had sold out and, with his brother and one or two other male relatives, had bought this valley. His family had come originally from the area, and we were forever meeting people who told us they were relatives of Señor Silva. He liked to talk to us, and on his first visit inevitably told us of the tragic German expedition and of the aeroplane that had crashed into the side of Yerupaja. He was also able to tell us about the Bonatti expedition, with details of their climb on Rondoy.

The only other climbing done that day was by Pete Farrell who soloed up a rock peak on the other side of the camp site from Ninashanca. For reference purposes, we called this rock peak 'Prince Philip'; it was meant as a joke, but the name stuck.

That night the eight of us were together in base camp for the first time in six days. We talked over the plans for Rondoy in the light of the climbing that had been done since we arrived. It was decided that someone ought to go up to investigate the descent onto the glacier seen by Charlie and Pete Westnidge. Graham and Pete Farrell volunteered to go up the next morning.

They set off at nine, up the moraine and across the terraces; nobody envied them the slog up those sections. Graham tired quickly and found the next sections a struggle, up the grass gullies, across the screes, and over the rock-pitches onto the ridge. Reaching the point from which Pete Westnidge and Charlie had seen the possible route onto the glacier, they descended down a rock-wall, leaving a fixed rope. From where they left the wall, they moved horizontally across a steep gully, half filled with snow. A good traversing line led them round the wall leading into the basin, until they found themselves on a ledge about sixty feet above the glacier. From this Pete Farrell abseiled down towards the glacier. At the end of the rope he found himself on a large ledge, from which he had to make the move onto the glacier itself. At this point the glacier side had crumbled into the bergschrund between the glacier and the rock-wall, providing a bridge across. Some twenty feet had to be gained through completely chaotic ice formations, and then a crevasse about a yard wide crossed, before the floor of the basin was reached. Graham watched from the top of the abseil point on the rock as Pete slowly made his way through this, the last obstacle to our access to the basin. Pete found no difficulty in negotiating the crevasse. This was the breakthrough, our first major problem solved. We now had a way into the ice-basin where we could establish a camp from which to make the attempt on Rondoy.

Pete looked around for a camp site, and then climbed back up the rock to where Graham was waiting. They left a fixed rope down the abseil wall, and another two along the traverse approaching the top of this point. They also built two cairns to mark the route, one at the beginning of the traverse from the ridge, and one at the top of the abseil into the gully seen by Pete Westnidge and Charlie. They made good time down to base camp, arriving back at five o'clock. I arrived a few minutes after them, having soloed up Prince Philip to take more photographs of Rondoy.

Pete Westnidge and Charlie had left for the Ninashanca camp a little before we arrived. They wanted to get some practice on snow and ice, and there were some convenient slopes close to the tent that we had left on Ninashanca. Dave Condict was to join them early the next morning, to help bring down the tent and other gear.

After we had eaten one of Pete Bebbington's justly famous Peruvian stews, Graham—who was feeling shattered by the heavy day—went off to his tent and began a marathon 'twelve-hour kip'. With the good news of a route into the ice-basin, spirits were running high; and the rest of us, Petes Bebbington and Farrell, Vic, Dave Condict, and myself, sat up yarning late into the night. It was Pete Bebbington's night. His tales of life in the Royal Navy were always guaranteed to keep us laughing for hours, and on this occasion he related his best. We were happy in each other's company and in the knowledge that tomorrow would really be beginning the first attempt of Rondoy.

5

The First Attempt

Dave Condict was up early the next morning to join Pete West-nidge and Charlie on Ninashanca. The rest of us spent the morning sorting out five or six hundredweight of food and equipment that had to be carried up into the ice-basin. This involved re-arranging the camp site in order to liberate the Dexion that we had used to support the sagging line. Pete Farrell, Vic, Graham, and Pete Bebbington were going to leave base camp that afternoon for the bivouac site at the foot of Rondoy Chico. The rest of us were to follow the next day, bringing the remains of the stores, while Pete Farrell and Vic loaded for a camp site in the basin, and Pete Bebbington and Graham carried stores up to them.

After a lazy afternoon, the four of them set off just as Charlie, Dave Condict, and Pete Westnidge arrived back from Nina-shanca. They had brought the tent and gear down from the Nina-shanca camp, for we had temporarily abandoned our not very serious attempts on Ninashanca, and the equipment would all be needed on Rondoy. The four of us in base camp watched the four members of the assault team making their way up the moraine. Pete Westnidge and I were getting the impression—wrongly, as it turned out—that the expedition was becoming exclusively for the more experienced climbers, while the rest of us were just acting as Sherpas. Charlie too was feeling sore, as there had never been any discussion as to who should be in the assault team. Those hard feelings disappeared as we watched them climb up the moraine with their enormous packs, Graham as usual having grabbed the heaviest. We busied ourselves preparing the evening meal which, however, gave us little satisfaction, for it was one of those meals during which everything possible goes wrong.

To start with, all the crockery, cutlery, and pots were dirty, having been forgotten in the day's rush. These now had to be taken down to the stream and washed with freezing water—an unpleasant job even in warm sunlight, but sheer hell in the dark, cold night. Dave Condict nobly volunteered to do it. Meanwhile Pete and I tried to make the stoves work. The two we used in base camp were both empty and now had to be filled in the dark, for naturally the Tilley lamp had chosen this night to give up the ghost. Once they were filled, both turned out to be blocked with carbon, and of course all the prickers had been taken 'up the hill' to the bivouac site. The stove we kept for emergencies became an emergency itself, for as soon as Pete put a match to it, the whole thing went up in flames. I picked it up and threw it through the tent door, and that was the end of that stove. Pete Westnidge is remarkably tolerant where people are concerned, seldom having a critical word for anyone. But he has a special, terrible, temper reserved for insects and inanimate objects. Candles that refuse to stand up, milk powder that just will not mix, rucksacks that don't fit properly, and ropes that snag, are inevitably treated to several minutes of intense cursing. A devout believer in the power of oaths to work miracles, he now directed his remarkable temper at the stoves. Subdued by the tirade, they gave in. To add to their humiliation Pete picked one up and lit his cigarette from it.

Charlie was the cook for the night. Normally, Charlie's stews were good and were always looked forward to. Tonight though, on top of everything else, it had to be a failure. He started by misjudging the amount of rice, so that when he opened the pressure cooker, half-cooked rice cascaded over the sides. It is a characteristic of rice that, if half-cooked to start with, it remains half-cooked despite all efforts to increase its cooking time. A stew based on half-cooked rice is never easy to digest. The stomach

pains which it manages to produce at 14,500 feet have to be experienced to be believed.

The drink at supper time was always something of a problem.
The question: 'What about a brew, then?' was sure to bring all the
possible replies: 'tea', 'coffee', 'chocolate', and 'Ovaltine'. Ovaltine was the expedition's favourite: so much so, that Pete Westnidge cracked that he was always surprised to find people still
awake for the second cup. As usual, it was after the decision had
been made and implemented that the big laughs came. In the
kitchen tent we all sat on biscuit-tins, and in one of them we kept
the sugar. This provided us with a game that might be called
musical biscuit-tins. The question 'who's on the sugar?', would be
met by silence. Then someone's nerve would break, and the rest
would all watch as he struggled up a few inches, his bowl of stew
in hand. In the crowded tent it required a great effort to lift yourself and raise the lid of the tin you had been sitting on. If it was
full of biscuits, you could sigh with relief: 'Not me'. If, however,
it was your seat that contained the sugar, you were involved in yet
another tricky operation: pressed against the wall of the tent, you
had to lean over, remove the tin and replace it with something
else. The second laugh over the sugar would come when Pete
Westnidge sweetened his drink. Pete has a sweet tooth and counts
his sugar by dessert spoons, not tea spoons.

We could see the lamps of the other four at the bivouac site as
they prepared their meal, and could at least feel comfortable compared with them. Their lights had also been seen by our farmer
friend, who came up the next morning, full of curiosity to know
how we were getting on. He had brought us news of the mules
we had asked him about, in anticipation of our move in August to
the other side of the range. We spent the morning talking to him
about South American politics.

Three o'clock in the afternoon saw the four of us starting out
with huge packs up the moraine. We were to meet Graham and

Pete Bebbington at the bivouac site—to which they would, by that time, have returned to spend the night—and go on up to the ice-basin the following morning. Arriving a little ahead of the others (I had started first), I dropped the heavy rucksack and lit a cigarette. Noticing that Pete and Graham were quiet, I asked them why. Whereupon Pete told me that they had, without thinking, taken all the paraffin up to the ice-basin, and that consequently we were faced with a night out with neither a hot evening meal nor a hot breakfast. The four of us who had just made the journey from base camp with heavy packs were not exactly pleased with this news. After a few sarcastic comments on some people's organizational genius, we turned about and raced back to base camp before dark.

Pete Bebbington and Graham had had a busy day. In the morning they had climbed with Vic and Pete Farrell up Rondoy Chico and traversed round to the abseil rope that dropped onto the glacier. Here they had been confronted with the problem of how to get their heavy packs across the crevasse and into the basin. It was out of the question to abseil down the rock and climb up the side of the glacier with the packs on. As usual Vic and Pete Bebbington came up with the solution. They fixed up an arrangement of ropes and karabiners from the rock-ledge at the top of the abseil wall, across the crevasse, to the glacier to which Pete Farrell had climbed across. One rope ran taut between a piton hammered into the rock and a piece of Dexion embedded in the ice, 120 feet away. The packs were then hung from this rope with karabiners. Another rope ran through two karabiners, one clipped onto a piton in the rock and one attached to the Dexion. The pack attached to this rope was hauled across the glacier by Pete Farrell at the Dexion end. The rope ran through a karabiner clipped onto the Dexion and then back up to the rock. This made it possible to return Pete B.'s and Graham's packs. The only snag in the system was due to the sag in the rope, which was as much as six feet where it reached the ice. The packs would come to rest against the side of the crevasse, and whoever was at the Dexion end would have to strain to pull them up to him. It was another of Vic and Pete Bebbington's brainchildren. They were the undisputed experts in the art of improvisation.

Pete Bebbington and Graham sent the packs across to Pete Farrell and Vic, and after collecting their own empty packs, they reversed the day's climbing, returning to the bivouac site. Pete Farrell and Vic stayed in the basin to find a camp site. This was something of a problem, for the basin was enclosed by a wall over 3,000 feet high—very steep, often vertical, and in places overhanging. Avalanches were continually falling away from the walls, their tracks converging on the floor of the basin which was covered with avalanche debris. Pete Farrell and Vic found a site at the back of the basin which seemed to be the only place completely free of avalanches. It was a platform about twenty feet wide and sixty across, beneath a small ice-wall.

Next morning, Sunday, July 21st, saw Pete Westnidge, Dave Condict, and myself once again making our way up the moraine, this time with light packs. Charlie Powell was left behind, assiduously looking after base camp. We arrived at ten-thirty at the bivouac site, where we found Pete Bebbington and Graham breakfasting. We arranged the stores into packs for the day's haul and discovered that there was too much for one trip: two of us would have to make the journey twice. We didn't give it much thought then, deciding to toss up later. A little apprehensive over the size of the packs, which must have been about 70 lb, we sat smoking for a while before setting off at midday. We traversed round the foot of the face across the top of some scree slopes to the grass gullies. These gullies were very steep, averaging between 70 or 80 degrees, and took a lot of hard climbing. Although the distance was only 200 feet or so, we straggled; and we were still quite spread out by the time the route grew level. Those in the lead waited here for the rest so that nobody would lose the route. Dave Condict had fallen behind owing to trouble with his awkward pack. Pete Bebbington, with characteristic unselfishness, changed packs with him, and we continued on up. Graham had marked the route with yellow chalk, so there was little possibility of anyone getting lost. But, in fact someone did: Graham!

Above the grass slopes we crossed a series of scree platforms, broken with small rock steps that we climbed by means of gullies that were presumably carved out by melt-waters. The highest scree slope was also the largest; it was 200 feet across, the top part being a permanent snowfield. It was here that Graham went off route. The snow led up to a rock-wall where, missing his own chalk marks, he found himself on a difficult rock-pitch. Pete Westnidge had followed him while I waited for Pete Bebbington and Dave Condict. Pete soon remembered the right route and shouted up to Graham who was, however, too much occupied with immediate problems to be able to reverse and follow us. The route proper lay up a series of chimneys, which gave some entertaining climbing with the huge and awkward packs we carried. It began to sound like a week-end in the Llanberis Pass as Pete Bebbington and I cursed our ways up, with ice-axes, sacks, and boots constantly jamming. The chimneys led us round to the right until, coming over the top of the last one, I found Peter sitting by a cairn, with nobody else in sight. From here we traversed round a couple of hundred feet to the second cairn. This pitch was on a steep wall of rotten rock, and in places the climb lay along a very thin and delicate ledge. The rock, falling away to several hundred feet below us, provided some exciting moments. At one point the handhold I was using came away and tumbled down to the glacier below. For a moment or two I thought that I was going to follow it. But I managed to regain my balance, while Pete watched me nervously.

At the second cairn we waited for the others. Graham was the first to appear, looking a bit bothered after his epic pitch of rock climbing. He gratefully sat down for a smoke while we watched Pete Westnidge make the traverse. Then Graham and Pete

Bebbington went off down the fixed-rope abseil to set up the pulley system, while Pete Westnidge and I waited for Dave Condict. When Dave appeared Pete Westnidge went after the others, closely followed by myself. The abseil down the gully from the cairn would have been easy enough had it not been for our packs. Using the rope to balance from, we descended 100 feet down a succession of small rock-ledges. This led right into the gully that split the face and was itself split into two sections by a ridge running down the middle. The first section was across rock and grit leading to a patch of hard snow covering the ridge. To a large extent the snow could be avoided, since a few steps across the top of it brought the traverse into the second section and back onto rock. Here we were brought to an abrupt halt up against a triangular flake, fifteen feet high. This was negotiated by the others by jamming up and down the crack between the flake and wall; this method was difficult for me, being six-feet-four, and I found it easier to straddle across the crack. Beyond this the route became rather delicate, and I for one was grateful to find that most of it had been supplied with fixed ropes the day before.

The others came into view as I traversed round a block of rock that jutted out from the wall. Graham was already on the glacier tightening the pulley ropes. Pete Westnidge and Pete Bebbington were doing the same from the rock end. It was an ardous task, and both Petes were puffing and blowing. Meanwhile Dave Condict arrived. The main ledge was crowded by the two Petes and all our packs, so Dave Condict and I had to perch uncomfortably around the corner on a tiny ledge, watching the antics of the others.

We had all arrived by one-thirty, and at first everything went so well that Pete Bebbington was continually chuntering: 'Very good, Robin Hood'—one of his favourite phrases. And then, as the first pack began its journey, the ropes twisted. The conversation degenerated. The pack was firmly stuck, fifty feet from the ledge and seventy feet from Graham. It hung unmoving over the crevasse. Pete Bebbington yelled to Graham to pull harder.

Graham pulled harder. 'The other rope,' Pete shouted. Graham pulled the other rope. Nothing happened. Pete untied one of the ropes and tried to untangle it. Graham tried again, but still with no success. But the untangling had been enough to free the rope between the ledge and the pack, and Pete managed to pull the pack back to the ledge. An hour had passed and we had got no-where. Dave Condict and I, perched on our ledge, were a little worried now, for we were watching the sun going down behind Ninashanca. Graham was already in the shadow and wearing his Duvet. We calculated that we too would be in the shadow by three o'clock, and our worry was that, as we had not expected to be out so long, neither of us, or Pete Westnidge, had brought our Duvets. Nor did we feel happy at the prospect of finding our way down to the bivouac in the dark.

Once the ropes were untangled it wasn't long before the first pack was on the ice and Graham was unloading it, while the two Petes pulled the karabiner back. The second gave no difficulty either, and this time the first pack came back empty. The second pack was Pete Bebbington's and—as he was staying here—it didn't have to be unloaded. By now the sun had disappeared and Dave and I were shouting encouragements, as we crouched shivering. The fourth pack seemed to be going across efficiently until the rope began to sag and the pack came up against the crevasse directly below Graham. The friction between the pack and the broken ice was immense and no efforts on Graham's part could move it. Graham took off his Duvet, despite the cold. Encouraged by remarks from us, he heaved away, but to no avail: the pack refused to budge.

Three of the packs having gone across, there was now a little more room on the ledge, so I moved round to help the two Petes at the rock end. Pete Westnidge and I pulled the rope through the karabiner in an attempt to make it taut. As Graham could not see the pack from his end, Pete Bebbington had to shout directions to him as to which way to pull. This too failed. Finally we decided that the three of us at our end would suddenly jerk the rope to make it taut, and also in the hope that the jerk would free the pack, when Graham could pull in from his end. This called for split-second timing, and the first two attempts finished with the pack back in the same position. On the third attempt Graham pulled at the right moment, and the pack moved a couple of feet nearer the top of the crevasse. Once again we jerked and pulled, and this time it was close enough to Graham for him to reach over and hold on to it. Lying flat on the ice he held onto the Dexion with one hand and slowly edged the pack up towards himself with the other. In the moment of triumph, as he dragged it over the top, we all cheered. Only one pack to go! But by now we had learnt something, and this time the three of us on the ledge pulled like hell when the pack neared the other side of the crevasse. As soon as he saw us jerk, Graham pulled too. Two of these jerk-and-pull movements, and the pack was safe.

Graham suddenly shouted that he could see Pete Farrell and Vic on the ice-face, about 100 feet below the ridge. He said that they seemed to be moving very slowly, probably because they were looking for a route as they climbed up to the ridge. This news cheered us tremendously. Graham emptied the other packs and sent them back. Pete Bebbington began to abseil down to the glacier to join Graham. The three of us who were going back—Pete Westnidge, Dave Condict and myself—wished them luck for the attempt, and then started on our way down. Pete and Dave Condict would be up again the next morning with the remaining loads, for I had won the toss and was going down to base camp. With Pete acting as pace-maker we raced along the route we had struggled up earlier, being back at the bivouac site in thirty-five minutes. As we hadn't planned to spend the night out we were not well supplied with bivouac gear, so leaving what I had behind for the other two I continued on to base camp in the failing light. The whole journey, from the ledge back to base camp, took me just over an hour.

24. Dave Condict on the ice-face, approaching the half-way
overhang

25. Pete Farrell on the rib running up to the north summit

26. On the first pitch of the traverse from the top of the rock-gully to the ice-gully leading to the snow-cave

27. The second pitch

Charlie was surprised to see me arriving on my own. He had expected all three of us, and had prepared a meal accordingly. It was up to his usual standards of stew, and very welcome. He had also made a bucket of thick custard. We ate as much as we could of both, leaving the rest as a basis for the following night's meal.

At the bivouac site, meanwhile, Pete and Dave were having problems. They discovered that they had no spoons, the most essential part of expedition equipment. Pete had to eat his stew with the top of a corned-beef tin, while Dave managed somehow with the silver paper used to keep tins of powdered food airtight. They had no airbeds, and spent a restless night, Pete continually being disturbed by the noise coming from the glacier about twenty feet away. It creaked and groaned all night, cracking loudly as pieces of ice broke away.

After we three had left, Pete Bebbington and Graham followed Vic's footsteps across the basin. They were surprised when they found the tent that Vic and Pete Farrell had put up the previous day, in a magnificent site, at the foot of the small ice-cliff. They put up beside it the tent that they had taken with them. They left at the pulley most of the loads that the five of us had taken up, to be ferried across the basin in the morning. Pete Farrell and Vic re-appeared on the face, coming out of a gully in which they had been hidden from view. They were moving very slowly, abseiling at times. Pete Bebbington and Graham began to prepare a meal for them. They discovered that the paraffin stoves were choked up and not working, and that all the prickers had been left at the bivouac site. Always the efficient camper, Pete Bebbington saved the situation by pulling a gas stove out of his rucksack. After dark, Pete Farrell and Vic arrived back at the tents from the ice-face, both looking completely shattered. They described how the face consisted of very steep snow and ice, from sixty to eighty degrees, and how the ridge was heavily corniced, and seemingly composed entirely of rotten ice. They were all quite happy to crawl into their sleeping-bags after the meal. Pete Bebbington had a rough night, for his airbed had developed a leak and was continually in need of blowing up.

The following morning, while Pete Farrell and Vic slept, and Pete Bebbington began to ferry yesterday's loads across the basin, Graham decided to go all the way back down to base camp to pick up another airbed for Pete, and his own inner sleeping-bag. Half way down he passed Pete Westnidge and Dave Condict on their way up. Weighed down under the packs of stores, these two passed some comments on Graham's reasoning powers, as he gaily tripped down the face. At the base camp, Charlie and I were greatly surprised to see him stride in off the moraine. While we made him lunch he gave us an account of Vic and Pete Farrell's climbing of the day before. After a short rest he started out for the ice-basin once again, with a spare ice-axe (to replace one broken on the face the previous day), a replacement for Pete Bebbington's airbed, and his own inner sleeping-bag. He also carried a message from Charlie to Pete Bebbington on how to rearrange the summit party to include Charlie.

Soon after Graham left, Dave Condict and Pete Westnidge arrived. They told us that when they had reached the ledge with the pulley they had whistled into the basin, and attracted Pete Bebbington's attention. The three in the tents went across to them to collect their packs, passing on Vic and Pete Farrell's description of the face and ridge. Then Pete and Dave came straight down to base camp, stopping only to pick up odds and ends from the bivouac site. They told Charlie and me that the four in the ice-basin—Vic, Graham, and Petes Bebbington and Farrell—were to make the attempt on Rondoy the following morning, leaving the ice-basin at 2 a.m. We spent the rest of the day sitting around reading and talking.

That evening after supper we heard the sounds of a storm approaching from the Amazon. Later still the valley began to be lit up by flashes of lightning. We wondered how the four in the basin were feeling, and hoped that the storm would soon pass.

The First Attempt

In the morning we woke to find the camp site covered with two or three inches of snow, and it was still snowing heavily. We assumed that the summit attempt was off. Even so we didn't envy them up in the basin. The weather had completely broken. The clouds hung low over the camp, sometimes dropping down to envelop it completely, so that we had difficulty in seeing across the site. The frieze of mountains at the head of the valley was quite invisible, though occasionally the air currents would burrow a way through the clouds and open a view of a ridge or peak. It was an eerie, impressive sight when the peak of Rondoy emerged at the end of one of these 'tunnels', outlined against a clear blue sky. Later in the morning the snow turned to sleet, hail, and then rain, reversing the pattern of the evening. By midday my tent was flooded at one end to a depth of two inches. With two tents up in the basin, I had had to move into the food tent, which was *not* the most weatherproof. Every hour or so I had to manœuvre myself out of my sleeping-bags, burrow between the boxes and sacks, and bail out the water with a sardine tin. Muffled up with Duvet jacket and Duvet socks, in a tent battered by the elements, I felt a sympathetic understanding as I read Robert Graves' account of his experiences of the trenches in the first world war.

The four of us spent the day reading, someone every now and then braving the blizzard to brew a drink. After supper we even mustered enough enthusiasm for an argument. The subject of the argument was the pay and conditions of work of English miners compared with Welsh miners. Charlie Powell argued, forcibly, that the English miners were overpaid and 'had it easy', while the rest of us took the opposite line. The argument was heated, probably due to the frustrating waste of a day, and finished with everyone storming back to their tents and their books.

The night before, midnight had seen Graham waking up in the basin and lighting the stove for breakfast. Putting his head out of the tent, he discovered the sleet and low cloud, and after they had

had a drink, they decided to go back to bed. At seven-fifteen the sleet had turned to heavy rain, and the day's climbing was called off. Graham made the breakfast and then continued to coax the only working stove into giving enough heat to melt ice for drinks. Graham had forgotten to take a book up with him, so while the others passed the time reading he had to sit twiddling his thumbs and nursing the stove. He was all the more tense because of a huge festering sore on his upper lip. When Pete Bebbington began to pester him to take the drink off and make him some milk and Weetabix, he had had enough: feeling surly with everyone he retired to his own part of the tent. He began to bring his diary up to date, but, running out of paper, he let Pete Farrell go back to his book and took over the stove again. Pete Bebbington offered to tear his own book—*Tales of Elizabethan Mariners*—in half and let Graham read it too; but never having been in the Navy, Graham didn't share Pete's enthusiasm. It snowed, rained or hailed all day, and by nightfall it was obvious that the attempt was off for the next day too. Even so Graham, ever hopeful, set his alarm for midnight, and when it went off looked out, to find that it was still snowing.

The next morning in base camp, while the four in the ice-basin camp were preparing to come down, Charlie was trying to persuade Pete Westnidge to join him in an attempt on Jirishanca Chico. Pete thought that the weather was too uncertain, and that conditions on the glaciers and snowfields would be too dangerous. The camp site was, indeed, covered with snow, and the cloud-bank was ominous. It had stopped snowing; but the wind and cold persisted, and occasionally the peaks would disappear in the mist. Later on it began to clear up a little and Pete agreed to go up the next day if the improvement continued.

We had another visit from our farmer-cum-landlord friend who promised us that the weather would be clear in the morning. He told us that he had come up to the lake because two of his cows had fallen in and one had frozen to death. The other he had managed to pull out, though this had involved sending his young brother into the lake to put the rope round the animal's head. He commented that the German expedition in 1951 must all have been '*loco*', for apparently they used to take a bath in the lake every morning. He told us that he had taken advantage of being near the camp to call in and invite one of us to go shooting with him on Peruvian Independence Day, July 28th, in four days' time.

In the afternoon the assault party came down from the ice-basin camp, partly to save food and other stores, and partly because—after the fall of fresh snow—a day's sun would be needed to melt the loose surface layer and a night's frost to harden any that failed to melt. It was Pete Bebbington's twenty-sixth birth-day; he had hoped to celebrate it by standing on the summit of Rondoy, and here he was back in base camp.

Charlie and Pete Westnidge decided after supper to start out for Jirishanca Chico the next morning. And as the assault party were planning to be back in the ice-basin the day after that, Dave Condict didn't see the prospect of any climbing in the next four or five days. He decided to walk back to Chiquian, taking and collecting mail. His basic motive was to find out whether or not he had passed his finals. Once he made this decision everyone spent the rest of the evening writing letters home.

About noon the next day Charlie and Pete Westnidge left for Jirishanca Chico with sufficient supplies for three nights out, since Pete Bebbington had calculated that it would take three days' climbing to reach the summit. The weather by now having completely cleared, they left the camp in blazing sunlight, while the other six of us were sun-bathing and swatting the flies that had returned with the sun. Pete Bebbington spent the afternoon fishing, and returned at tea-time with an enormous rainbow trout, fourteen inches long and weighing about $4\frac{1}{2}$ lb. Pete told us that he had had three bites, but the other two were so big that he just looked at them in amazement and let them escape. At the time, we looked a bit dubious, but later we were to see for ourselves trout of over two feet long. The story goes that in an effort to balance the highland Indian's diet, the authorities decided to stock the Andean rivers and lakes with trout. Having done so, they forgot to teach the Indians how to fish, with the result that the trout have grown, uninhibited, to enormous sizes. The only people we found who did take advantage of these fish were the farmer and his family, and they were not exactly underfed Indians.

The trout provided the six of us with an ample portion each which Pete Bebbington cooked superbly. We celebrated the catch by eating it with chips fried in an open pressure cooker, which we followed by Christmas pudding and Vic's custard. After the meal we sat round in the candle-light talking. Pete Farrell, who was seldom quiet, kept us laughing with tales of climbing in New Zealand; and Vic, who normally says very little, added his stories too. It turned into a joke session; and the constant laughter, added to the discomfort of crouching on biscuit-tins, did little to help the digestive systems after the onslaught they had sustained. Most of us spent a rough night.

Early next morning Dave Condict set off for Chiquian and, as we watched him slog up the ridge, nobody envied him his journey. He had one consolation: he would arrive in Chiquian in time for the Independence Day celebrations. The fiesta was reputed to be worth taking part in. Many local Indians would be travelling to Chiquian for the celebrations, which for them would consist mainly of heavy drinking.

Encouraged by the previous day's sun, the four who were in the Rondoy party decided that conditions would be right for climbing the face. As the weather was continuing perfect they packed and set off up the moraine after lunch. I reconciled myself to what I expected to be three days alone in the camp, and began to pass the time by bringing my diary up to date. Late in the afternoon I was surprised by shouts, and wondered who it could be. I shouted back, but couldn't see anyone. The shouts continued and suddenly I saw a figure waving from the last direction that I could have expected. Someone was descending the grass slopes above the lake, *down* the valley. As it was on the Jirishanca Chico side of the valley I knew it must be either Pete Westnidge or Charlie, but I couldn't make out which, until—with the telescope—I saw that it was Pete. I was worried lest there had been an accident, as Pete was moving very fast. Then Charlie appeared on the ridge and shouted too, moving very slowly and at least an hour behind Pete. It turned out that he had, unknown to Pete, tripped in some *puna* grass and twisted his ankle.

I had some soup and Ovaltine ready for Pete by the time he arrived, and while we watched Charlie make his way down he told me about their day's climbing.

When they left the base camp they had followed the route up to Prince Philip, at first up the steep lateral moraine on the opposite side of Ninashanca from the moraine that gave access to Rondoy. From the top of the moraine the route lay up very steep scree slopes at the side of Prince Philip. Even without a pack I had found the scree slopes hard going; but Pete and Charlie, carrying 50 lb apiece, found them absolutely desperate. Skirting round three snowfields they gained height rapidly. At the top of the scree they moved into a gully running round the back of Prince Philip. This gave access to the shoulder between Prince Philip and the knife-edge ridge leading to the summit of Jirishanca Chico. The rock in the gully was rotten and crumbled away rapidly as they climbed. Pete described it as 'real nightmare stuff'. At the top of the gully was a snowfield, leading to the shoulder. Charlie went onto and up the snowfield for a while and then suddenly traversed out onto the rock. After some strenuous climbing they reached the crest of the knife-edge ridge, hauling their sacks up on the rope over the steeper pitches. The ridge was a true knife edge (see Plate 15) dropping away sharply on both sides. It was now about five-thirty and night was approaching fast. For a bivouac spot, they found a rectangular rock ledge just below the summit of the ridge with ample room for two airbeds. The ledge fell away 1,000 feet onto the glacier, across which was a spectacular view of Rondoy. From this vantage point they could see clearly that Rondoy had two major peaks, one of which was not visible from base camp. Between the two peaks they could see a snow-ridge. This was the heavily corniced, dangerous ridge that the Italians had written of as hopeless, when it stopped their attempt on the south summit.

Pete and Charlie's bivouac site boasted a patch of snow running between the airbeds, which acted as their water supply. They had a cold but good night, the alarm rousing them at 4 a.m. At six forty-five they climbed back to the ridge, which they hoped would give the lead onto the summit. A closer inspection—made possible by the morning light—shattered this belief. The ridge was very long and very steep, alternating most of the way between bare rock, and rock covered with a thin layer of snow. It led into a succession of three overhanging ice-walls, which it seemed impossible to avoid.

They decided that their best chance lay on the east ridge: the back skyline ridge on the left of Plate 15. They descended down the far side of their ridge, and crossed the snowfield lying between them and the col which joined the east ridge of Jirishanca to a minor peak to the east. Two rope-lengths up from the snowfield, in a gully leading to the col, they found themselves forced onto incredibly bad rock. As the gully was in fact a stone shoot, excitement was added to the already difficult climbing by boulders of all sizes that whistled down continually.

The snow leading from the col up the east ridge was in excellent condition, so they made good time. Then abruptly, about 400 feet from the summit, the snow ran out, giving way to the characteristic rotten red rock. At first they were exhilarated by the sight of the summit so close to them, feeling that it was definitely 'in the bag'. But when they started to climb they discovered that the rock offered no natural, secure belay-point, and tried to hammer in a piton. But the rock was so loose that it simply would not hold a piton. Working out the possibilities, Charlie took up a tension stance, bracing himself amongst some loose blocks and belaying round a loose flake. Pete edged himself out onto the ridge about fifteen feet above Charlie and began to pick his way up. Every move required ten minutes thought, involving the removal of loose rock before each move, and usually some more during the move. The loosened rock fell away to the left, bouncing down a rock gully to the glacier 2,000 feet below.

Pete tried to see whether or not it was possible to traverse out onto the face and into one of the two snow gullies leading to the summit. These gullies were about 100 yards away on either side of the ridge and would have involved climbing across rock similar to that of the ridge, with even less protection. He shouted down to Charlie a report of what he could see and they decided to give up the attempt.

They came down to base camp, following a route on the other side of the ridge that divided the base camp valley from the next, coming over the ridge where it involved no climbing. Pete Westnidge later said that any route to that side (the east) of Jirishanca Chico looked quite hopeless: sooner or later you would have to move onto that rotten rock. From where they were camped the only possibility would be the knife-edge north ridge that Charlie and he had thought looked desperate; and that would be a really hard climb.

The next day, July 27th, was my twenty-third birthday, marked only by a special breakfast, for which we had the remains of the previous night's stew as a change from the usual Weetabix and milk. When we emerged from the cocoons of our sleeping-bags in the morning we saw two ropes of two, high on the face of Rondoy. We worked out that they must have started out not long after midnight. Through the telescope we could make out that Pete Farrell and Vic were in the lead, cutting steps. We spent the morning watching their progress up the face until, at midday, they disappeared over the ridge. Or, at least, until they *seemed* to disappear over the ridge, for we later discovered that they had disappeared *into* the ridge.

During that afternoon I lost large numbers of cigarettes to Pete, who had become very adept at a Peruvian dice game. We also prepared between us an enormous meal of solids instead of the usual stew. Although the meal—soup, fried onions, meat, chips, and beans, followed by Christmas pudding and custard—was fabulous to *eat*, it was absolute hell to digest. All three of us spent most of the night in suffering. Sleeping in a tent with Pete Westnidge involved sharing his habits, the most important of which was to wake up in the middle of the night for a hot drink, smoke, and chat. If, when Dave Condict and Pete Westnidge were both in base camp, you woke up between two and three in the morning, you could be sure to hear mumbling and laughter coming from their tent. That night, however, I was grateful when Pete suggested a smoke. It came as a relief from the sleeplessness and stomach pains.

The next day, Sunday, July 28th, was Peruvian Independence Day, and we sat waiting for the farmer to appear with his gun. In the middle of the morning Pete suddenly shouted that he could see something moving near the north summit. For a while neither Charlie nor I could see what he was pointing to, and then we saw an ice-axe flashing in the sun. With the telescope we made out that it was Vic. Soon Pete Farrell appeared and, as they traversed round under the summit, yet another figure. For a while we were puzzled, for we could never see more than three people at a time; then we worked out that the route spiralled round as it gained height on the ice-cone that capped the north summit. As one person disappeared, another would soon come into view. They seemed to be moving very slowly, and it was noon before they reached the summit.

It must be explained that we all believed the summit climbed that day to be the south, and highest, summit; because it was both the highest visible from base camp and the one seemingly lying furthest to the south. We assumed that, if there was another summit behind, it would be lower. The consequence was that we, down in base camp, thought that they had climbed the highest point on Rondoy. But it is obvious from Graham's diary that they were really on the north summit, though they themselves believed that they were on the south. Even though they could see that the other summit—which came into view from the one they had just climbed—was a few hundred feet higher, they still referred to it as the north summit.

Convinced that Rondoy had been climbed, nobody felt like doing anything; and while the other two went off fishing, I had a bath in the stream. The farmer arrived complete with gun while I was drying. As Charlie was nowhere to be seen we went off together to hunt *viscatcha*. The *viscatcha* was the most common form of animal life in the valley, a grey rodent something like a squirrel in appearance, but with actions and habits like a rabbit. We had also occasionally seen a quick-footed variety of deer higher up the moraine. Apart from mice which lived with me in the food tent, the only other wild life we found in the valley were the birds. These ranged from eagles and condors, down to tiny mustard-coloured birds which, being gregarious by nature, always flew in large flocks. In looks and habits they were something between a great-tit and a sparrow, and were always hanging around the camp site for titbits.

The farmer, his single-barrelled shotgun slung over his shoulder, set off with me up the moraine. I led him towards the group of boulders where we had often seen the *viscatcha*, and sure enough we came across one. It was about ten feet away, camouflaged against the grey rock. I stopped the farmer with a touch on his arm.

'Where?', he whispered.

'There,' I said, pointing, 'about three metres directly in front of you.'

'I can't see it,' he said, 'I have broken my glasses and can only see in blurs. *You* will have to point the gun.'

Rondoy

The animal looked at us in amazement as I pointed the shotgun for the farmer and, not liking the look of what was going on, he turned tail. But unfortunately for him, he turned round after a few feet to see if he could really believe his eyes. That was the last thing he did, for the farmer had seen the movement and fired at it. The explosion echoed around the valley with a tremendous roar, and the *viscatcha* jumped once and then lay dead.

On the way down to base camp the farmer told me one of his secrets—how to judge the tenderness of a *viscatcha*'s meat. He wrapped the end of the long bushy tail round his finger and pulled, whereupon the top of the tail came off bringing with it a long spinal cord. The length of the cord, he told me, varied with the tenderness of the meat. Apparently ours would be very tender indeed. Back in base camp we exchanged news over a cup of tea. I told him of the 'ascent of Rondoy', on which he congratulated us. His news was of the agreement abolishing H-bomb tests for two years. I mused on his enthusiasm and earnestness about it; for a farmer living 14,000 feet up in the Peruvian Andes was the last person I should have expected to be giving the Bomb any thought at all. He also told us that he had met the Spanish expedition that morning. Apparently they had climbed Nevada Siula, a peak of over 20,000 feet to the east of Yerupaja, and were now leaving the Huayhuash.

After he left the camp, the farmer came across Charlie and Pete Westnidge on their way back from three hours' fruitless fishing. Charlie arranged to go shooting with the farmer in four days' time. Charlie gutted the *viscatcha* and we made a stew out of it; it tasted very much like a rabbit, only richer. The meal over, we sat talking. Charlie and Pete decided to go off the next morning to make the fourth attempt on Ninashanca. Disappointed after Jirishanca Chico they were both determined to make an all-out effort on Ninashanca; but especially Charlie, for whom it would be the second attempt.

6

Interlude

Shortly after noon the following day, Monday, July 29th, Pete Westnidge left the base camp with Charlie for the fourth attempt on Ninashanca. At about the same time, the four on Rondoy—Pete Farrell and Vic, Pete Bebbington and Graham—appeared over the ridge and began to descend the face into the ice-basin. I remember that day well, for after Pete and Charlie disappeared over the top of the ridge opposite the base camp, I sat and watched the setting sun catch the snow-capped peaks of Jirishanca. It was a rare day, no clouds having found their way up from the Amazon, and the ridge of the Huayhuash was silhouetted against the deepening blue sky. I remembered how Vic had said a few days earlier what a good job somebody had made in cutting out the sky to put on top of the ridge, so that it fitted perfectly.

I was musing away the afternoon when I was suddenly roused from my thoughts by shouting. At first I thought that it was Dave Condict, back from Chiquian. But nothing was moving in that direction. Then I noticed two figures at the top of the river valley that ran down the side of the moraine. I assumed that the Rondoy party had made good time down the face and had decided to come right down to base camp. So I brewed a hot drink, put the meal on, and went out to meet them. It turned out to be only the two Petes—Graham and Vic having both decided to stay up in the basin for the night.

Over the meal Pete Bebbington gave me his account of the second ascent of Rondoy North, for by then we had worked out that it must be the north summit, the one Bonatti had already climbed. The four of them had started off from the ice-basin

95

camp at 2.30 a.m. on July 23rd. The alarm had gone at midnight, but it had taken two and a half hours to make the breakfast and other preparations. At first Pete Bebbington and Graham had found themselves a little stiff, but after an hour or so they had warmed up and picked up speed. Pete Farrell and Vic were in the lead making the route. The face was steep but the snow condition was good, as was the weather, and they made reasonable time. The middle of the face was marked by a prominent overhang (see Plate 18) which provided a resting place; this they reached by dawn. From here the face steepened, and Vic and Pete Farrell (on their earlier climb) had cut a series of steps, zig-zagging up. A traverse under the line of the ridge, across a series of steep ribs and gullies, brought them into a final steep gully of loose rock which formed the east upper extreme point of the face. From the top of it Vic saw a traverse line that led through the chaotic formations of broken ice. The climbing eventually became so difficult that each 100 feet took three hours.

The first sixty feet, however, was a relatively easy traverse along a foot-wide ledge (see Plate 26). The ice was extremely hard and the crampon points would not bite. The ledge petered out on a steep broken section (see Plates 27 and 28 of Pete Farrell leading this section). From there, the route led up, across, and into an even steeper ice-gully, eight feet wide and sheering away thousands of feet to the glacier below. Vic, who now was leading, solved the problem of the gully with a superb piece of artificial climbing technique. He drove an ice-piton into the ice for Pete Farrell to use as a belay. Then, digging in his crampons, he leant out almost horizontally on a tight rope from Pete and hammered in a second peg. From this he took his tension as he swung his feet round to below him, and kicked in the front points of his crampons. Leaning out left again he hammered in a third piton far enough out to be able to swing across onto a tiny ice-ledge, using a sling which he had clipped into the piton. The ledge led across the remaining three feet to the other side of the gully.

Interlude

He traversed round the corner into another steep ice-gully. At full rope-length he hammered in the longest piton he had for a belay. Between his legs, he could see down to the ice-basin and base camp. He looked around for a weakness in the wall above that would give him access to the ridge or provide shelter for the night.

In the almost vertical gully, the ice was rotten and very brittle. In one way, the rottenness of the ice helped, by providing an occasional foothold. Vic climbed up sixty feet to just below the crest of the ridge, and saw a small hole in the ice. Peering through he found an ice-cave that the wind had burrowed right through the ridge. The problem of the bivouac site was solved.

He enlarged the 'door' and climbed in, finding that he could stand upright inside. Eight feet away on the other side another 'door' led out onto the opposite face. Outside it was a ledge two feet wide and ten feet long, and then the face dropped away abruptly for several thousand feet. Inside, the cave was in two parts; an upper part leading from one entrance to the other, about three feet wide and eight feet long, and a lower part sloping into the ice for eight feet. A sharply sloping roof lessened the value of the lower section, but all-in-all the cave provided an admirable bivouac site, almost completely sheltered from the elements.

Vic screwed in an ice-piton for a belay and brought Pete Farrell up, followed by Pete Bebbington and Graham. By the time they were all in the cave it had taken six hours to climb the last 200 feet. The whole day's climbing had taken fifteen hours. After admiring the views, on one side down the Pacclon valley towards Chiquian and the *Puna*, and on the other down the base camp valley across the foothills towards the Amazon, they settled down to a meal cooked on the ledge, which had become the kitchen. They spent an uncomfortable night, for lying on ice without airbeds or sleeping-bags is a misery. They arranged the ropes and sacks as best they could to provide some protection, but everybody still suffered from the cold. Apart from cold feet,

Graham was also having trouble with his eyes, for during the day his snow-goggles had been hurting him and he had occasionally taken them off for greater immediate comfort.

After the miserable night nobody seemed keen on an early start, and it was seven-thirty before they left the cave by the opposite door to the one they had entered. A steep pitch directly above the cave led onto the ridge. The route up the ridge was blocked by a dangerous-looking ice-bridge and they descended an easy pitch down the east face to avoid it. (It was here that they became visible to us in base camp.) From the bottom of this pitch they traversed left and down a ramp for 150 feet until they were directly beneath the north summit. Pete Farrell led the next pitch up and across broken ice; it was hard going and, to us in camp, he seemed to be hardly moving. Meanwhile the others waited below. Eventually Pete Farrell shouted down that he was belayed, whereupon Vic climbed up to the belay stance and then led through. We watched Vic from base camp through the telescope as he cut steps up the last pitch to the summit, and then the others as they climbed up to join him.

After a rest they continued along the ridge leading to the higher summit, which looked a disturbingly long way away. The ridge was difficult and narrow, covered with soft snow. Pete Farrell led up and over a bulge which brought him onto another stretch of ridge leading to an obviously difficult pitch of rock climbing. He followed this until he came up against a major obstacle in the shape of a rock-gendarme. At this point they decided to give up climbing for the day, and started to reverse their route towards the ice-cave. They abseiled down from the north summit. But the rope stuck; and after all efforts to remove it had failed, they left it there and continued their climb back to the ice-cave. To make this easier, they hammered a piece of Dexion into the ridge above the cave, and used it for protection on the twenty-foot descent down the west face to the ledge outside the cave.

By the time they reached the ice-cave it was completely dark.

28. The second pitch

29. Looking down the Pacclon valley from the ice-cave

Interlude

To make the night pass more quickly they took their time over preparing for bed. Then, during the night, Pete Bebbington woke up feeling thirsty, roused Graham too, and suggested brewing up. Graham lit a cigarette and began to make a drink of Oxo. He became irate when Pete said he would prefer lemonade which—since their only lemonade was in the water-bottles, frozen solid—would have taken about an hour longer. After this the night passed more comfortably than the one before.

The next morning Graham climbed back up to the ridge to retrieve the rope he had used to abseil down the previous night. This they used as a fixed rope to abseil down the gully immediately below the cave on the east side. They left both this rope and the rope along the traverse in position to save time on the next attempt. Another abseil down the rib of loose rock brought them onto the face proper. The climb down the face was long and arduous. They were all tired and moved slowly. In the process, three ice-axes and one North-Waller were broken, and one North-Waller lost. Below the rock-pitch leading round the lower bergschrund the snow was very soft, and movement became a progression of clumsy slides. At the tents they had a meal, after which Pete Farrell and Pete Bebbington decided to come right down to base camp.

Vic and Graham joined us in the middle of the following afternoon. We were hoping that Dave Condict would arrive from Chiquian during the day. When he still hadn't appeared by nightfall we gave him up, but not before Pete Bebbington had yelled some encouraging remarks into the placid night sky. At eight-thirty, when we were beginning to think of settling down for the night, Dave arrived out of the darkness. He entertained us for a while with tales of his eventful journey, before we settled down into our sleeping-bags to read the letters he had brought us. His own news was of his degree, which he had gained with Honours.

The next morning we sat in the sun exchanging outside news, mainly about the Christine Keeler affair and the Test Matches.

Rondoy

While Dave read his girl friend's account of the second Test, Pete
Bebbington and I walked backwards and forwards across the
camp site in an attempt to unravel the fishing line; for the only
outcome of Pete Westnidge's fishing expedition had been to snarl
it into a magnificent tangle. Graham was greasing his boots, Vic
and Pete Farrell were sunbathing and swatting flies. Suddenly we
heard a shout and, looking up, saw Charlie coming over the grass
ridge above the base camp. As he wandered down we wondered
where Pete Westnidge was, for normally Pete would have been
well in the lead. Charlie came into camp grinning apologetically,
to tell us that Pete had had an accident and was waiting up in the
Ninashanca high camp for a stretcher.

It appeared that Pete Westnidge had caught his crampon in his
snow-boot when jumping over a bergschrund, and had landed
with his foot twisted. His ankle was very swollen and was obviously badly sprained; but as he could still move it a little, he decided it could not be broken. (In fact, as he discovered eventually,
it had been broken in two places.)

As we believed Pete to be resting comfortably in the high
camp, we had a meal before setting out. Graham, who wasn't
feeling well, stayed in base camp. Six of us went: four to carry
Pete down on the stretcher, the other two to bring the packs
down from the camp site. Moving quickly, we arrived in about
an hour at the cattle gate, where the shoulder led up to the top of
the rock-wall. Here we were surprised to find Pete waiting for us.
Realizing that it would be almost impossible for us to carry him
down the rock sections, he had hobbled down as far as he could,
using an ice-axe for support.

Once again Vic and Pete Farrell's experience and skill became
evident as they quickly assessed the situation and made a stretcher
out of their superb New Zealand Mountain-Mule pack-frames
and two ice-axes, while Charlie and Dave Condict went up to the
camp site to collect the packs. Then Pete Farrell and Vic, Pete
Bebbington and I, took it in turns to carry Pete down the steep

slopes back to base camp. It was hard, hot work, but Pete kept us amused. He knew it would mean the end of his climbing on the expedition and was 'choked off no end', but he remained cheerful. It took us an hour and a half to reach base camp. From the top of the ridge overlooking the camp we shouted to Graham to put a brew on, and looking up he noticed two Indians, complete with shot-guns, sorting out the empty tins in our rubbish heap.

The broken ice-axes that Vic had brought down proved useful, for Pete Farrell made from them an excellent crutch for Pete, strengthening it with two tent-poles and a reel of tape. It became one of the sights of base camp to see him hobbling round on his crutch like Long John Silver.

The next day was designated as a rest day, Vic and Charlie being the only two who did anything at all. Vic went on a photographing expedition in an attempt to get all the three peaks of Rondoy into one photograph. Some of the results of that day's work illustrate this book. Charlie went off with the farmer in the afternoon, hunting *viscatcha*. They went out twice, once after midday and again after dusk; but as on each occasion they returned empty-handed, we were reduced to the traditional stew for supper.

In the afternoon Pete Westnidge gave the rest of us an account of his climbing on Ninashanca with Charlie. They had apparently pitched their camp much higher than the site used by the previous three parties. They pitched the tent twenty feet from the cornice, just below the main, north-west ridge. It was an exposed position, and their night had been disturbed by winds buffeting their tent. The wind continued through the night, and was so bitter that at four o'clock—when they had intended to start climbing—they decided to wait for the sun before venturing out. It was still bitterly cold in the wind, however, and they climbed wearing Duvets and three layers of trousers. One of the wind's better side-effects was to keep the snow in good condition. It was the loose snow that had slowed down the three previous attempts. They made a reasonable time up to the first of the crevasses where they stopped for a rest. Then they climbed up the upper wall of the crevasse by means of a delicate snow-bridge that led between the ice-wall and the organ-pipe-type icicles. This gave them access to the main face, at the top of which they were stopped short by the second crevasse. Pete began to lead up the back wall using pitons. Pete described how his 'attempt to peg (his) way up the soft ice of the back wall ended with (him) plonking on (his) backside at the bottom'. Understandably, they decided to find a way round the crevasse, rather than try to climb up it. They traversed three rope-lengths to the right of the wall, which led them onto the soft snow of the north face. The north face dropped away steeply to a lake 3,000 feet below. They traversed two rope-lengths across this, expecting at every step to slide away with the melting snow; then they climbed up vertically, bringing themselves back onto the rib above the crevasse. As they climbed up the next section they found themselves up against the wall of the third crevasse. This time the ice was too soft to hold pitons; and as the only two traverse routes led on the one hand into rotten ice and on the other into a succession of ice-walls, they decided to call off the attempt. They thought of descending down the face to the soft snow, continuing their traverse line to directly below the summit, and then climbing directly up. But they had lost their enthusiasm, and started to climb back down to the tent.

At the crevasse that they had traversed round on the way up, they decided to avoid the loose snow by jumping the twelve feet onto the platform below the icicles. Pete went first, catching his crampons in his overboots as he took off. He landed off balance and felt a tremendous pain in his left ankle. Sitting in the snow, he thought at first that he wasn't going to be able to walk on it, and would have to bivouac where he was until the stretcher party arrived. While he was musing along these lines Charlie had successfully jumped over the crevasse. He coaxed Pete into trying to stand on his foot, and they found that he could walk so long as he could keep his foot flat. This meant walking sideways down the slope, keeping the inner points of the crampons firmly embedded and level.

Pete led off back down to the high camp with Charlie keeping him on a tight rope. It was a painful process for Pete and a nerve-racking one for Charlie, who had to be constantly on the alert in case Pete should slip and lose his balance. They reached the tent in ten rope-lengths, with Charlie talking and joking all the way to keep up Pete's spirits. They were both very tired, and after a hurried meal went off to sleep quite easily.

They were up at seven-thirty the next morning and after breakfast Pete set off on his own, leaving Charlie to pack up the tent and load everything into his pack. The ankle had worsened during the night and Pete didn't feel too good. When Charlie caught up with him he was paddling down the last snow slope on his backside, the strain of walking upright having been too much. When Charlie saw this, he realized that Pete would have to be carried down to base camp. He dumped his pack, told Pete to rest where he was, and then raced down to tell the rest of us. After a short rest Pete decided to make his own way as far as he could, using an ice-axe for a walking-stick. It cost him considerable effort and he was glad to see us at the cattle gate when he arrived. But he was already half way down to base camp, and had solved our worst problem of getting him down the scree and rock slopes on a stretcher.

In base camp the ankle continued to worsen and it became obvious that as far as climbing went, the expedition was over for Pete.

As a result of the loss of three ice-axes on the east face, and the failure of the four new ones to turn up at Lima, we had no spares. Hence, if any more were lost or broken, we should find ourselves in difficulties. Pete Bebbington decided that the best thing would be to cable Colin Darbyshire, an English climber settled in Peru, and ask him for the loan of his ice-axes. There was no difficulty in getting them up to the Huayhuash, as we were to be joined the following week by Derek Fabian, an old friend of the L.S.E. club who had been invited earlier to come with us. Other commitments had prevented his taking part in the whole expedition, but he had promised to join us for the last three weeks in August. He had once worked in Lima, and we knew that he was a friend of Colin's and was bound to see him on his way through Lima.

When the farmer arrived to take Charlie shooting, we asked him where the nearest telegraph office was. He told us that Queropalca had one and was only an hour's walk beyond his house. Our only map seemed to confirm this by marking Queropalca about five miles from the base camp. Pete Bebbington decided to go down the next day; Pete Farrell, Vic, and I said we would go too, for the walk. The rest of that day passed with everybody writing letters.

We started out at nine next morning, first ambling down to the farmer's house to ask about the route and to say that we would call on the way back. He had invited us all to meet his family that day, and we told him that the others would be arriving in two hours, when we hoped to be back. He assured us that it would only take us an hour each way. We wondered later just how he worked that out, for the journey there and back took us five and a half hours of hard walking.

At first the valley was as boring as any other highland valley; but as we lost height it became more interesting. We were stopped by a very drunken, coca-chewing, Indian on horseback who complained bitterly about the election of Sr Belaúnde Terry as the Peruvian president. This area of Peru is very much a stronghold of Haya de la Torre, and this Indian seemed especially disappointed that he had not won the elections. He became quite heated, and we left him shouting that the elections had been rigged. We also came across many children, looking after animals;

but they ran away as soon as we approached. When we had been walking for two hours in the blazing sun we began to doubt the existence of Queropalca, and sat down to wait for an Indian riding towards us to check that we were on the right path. As he came nearer we realized that he wasn't guiding the horse, but letting it have its head. When we came close we could see that his huge eyes were staring ahead of him, completely sightless. It was strange to see him sitting bolt upright on his horse, with his fixed, expressionless face.

The few times that we managed to ask how far it was to Queropalca were little help, for each time we got answers that did not match up. The first person we asked told us that it was half a league away, and the next said a league and a half. We gave up enquiring after our last informant, a young boy, told us that it was: '*Circita—aqua no mas*', which means, translated literally: 'Very close—just here, no further.' But in fact it means 'Oh, miles yet'. The path for the last few miles was cobbled, in a primitive fashion, a welcome contrast to the dust we had been walking in. Pete Bebbington explained to us that Queropalca had once been an Inca silver-mining town. The hills round it are still reputedly rich in various metals, but lack of communications makes mining them too difficult. Along this 'metalled' stretch of road we found groups of Indian children from the village cutting peat, the only source of fuel during the bitter cold nights.

The path led up the slopes onto a plateau in the next valley. As we came round and approached the village we were surprised to see Yerupaja in the distance at the head of the valley. When we entered Queropalca it was much bigger than we had expected. We followed a stream of water which led us to the main piazza, a barren patch about fifty yards square complete with flagpole and Peruvian flag. The only sign of life was a dog, and that didn't seem to have much life left.

We found the post-office closed. A little boy who appeared from nowhere told us that it would be open in an hour and a half.

This was fine by us as long as we could meanwhile find something to eat and drink. We had no food with us, as we had expected to be back at base camp for lunch; and after the unexpectedly long trek in the hot sun and dust we were desperate for some refreshment. We asked the boy if he knew of a café. He looked at us in amazement, and laughed at the naïvety of the question. The inhabitants have difficulty enough in finding food for themselves, without maintaining a café. Even the bread has to be brought forty-five miles from Chiquian on mules, across the Kakanan Pass at 15,500 feet.

We next asked for beer, confident that there must be a stores where it was sold. He seemed to have been expecting this question, and with a little laugh led us off to the 'bar'. It was closed, of course. Undaunted, we went round the back to look for the owner. We found him in a yard full of dogs. On a washing line, strips of meat were hanging out to dry, and three old women walked about spinning wool. Vic and I were completely taken aback when, after we had asked for some beer, the shopkeeper answered us by our Christian names. He turned out to be the cousin of the farmer who had visited us in base camp, and on whose horse Vic and I had photographed each other. He opened up his shop for us and served us our beer. I noticed a tin of coffee on a shelf, and asked if he could make us some. This flummoxed him. First he had to send out a boy to find the village primus stove which, when it eventually appeared, I refused to believe would work. It must have been *the* original paraffin stove. But after being caressed and coaxed it showed signs of working. That is to say, it began to give off clouds of thick black smoke and then suddenly roared into flames. I thought that it had blown up, but this in fact was the stove at its most efficient.

While we waited for the coffee, we sent one of the many little Indian boys now crowding round the door to buy us a sack-load of bread rolls. When he returned with them, we made sandwiches of tinned tuna fish and sprats that we had bought. We ourselves very much appreciated eating them, while the whole village seemed to enjoy the spectacle.

At two o'clock we went round to the post-office, which was still closed. We sat down against the wall while someone went off to rouse the post-clerk from his siesta. While we were waiting we noticed that the village had been built along the banks of a small river which had been directed into a concrete channel running down the main street and one side of the square. Near to where we sat, the channel had been blocked, diverting the fast flowing water across the square. As a result the downslope half of the square was reasonably firm and boasted an occasional patch of tough grass, whereas the other half was of bare earth, covered with a layer of dust.

The clerk arrived and we shuffled into his 'office' to send off the telegram. The telephone receiver was a vintage model, and Vic and I left the two Petes to the delights of Andean telecommunications and went back out into the sunlight. While listening to the problems of the local schoolteacher, which all seemed to stem from the lack of women in Queropalca, we heard sounds of music. We were told that it was the village 'band' practising for the forthcoming fiesta to celebrate the tenth anniversary of the football pitch. We were taken into the house whence the music came and found two violinists and a harpist. The harp was a magnificent affair, set on a huge wooden sounding-box; these harps are the traditional musical instrument of the area. The room was completely bare except for two wooden frame-beds, on which Vic and I were invited to sit. When our eyes became accustomed to the gloom after the bright sun, we noticed in one corner an old woman buried under black blankets. Seeing us looking at her, one of the violinists snapped his fingers, and she ran out, rustling her many black skirts.

After a long tuning-up session the three musicians played their favourite Andean folk songs. Andean music is very pleasant, catchy with a regular beat, and soon everyone was tapping their feet. A little girl of three or four was pushed into the centre of the room and told to dance, just like any little English girl being told to twist. This child, however, was a wonderful little dancer of the traditional Peruvian dances, with their spins and twirls, and handkerchief-waving. While she was dancing, the two Petes came in. Pete Bebbington asked the musicians if they knew his favourite *huayno*, '*Destino Negro*', which is about the soul of a dying man flying over the mountains. It is a mournful piece and very beautiful. When I tried later in Lima to buy a recording I could find nobody who had even heard of it. I was surprised at this, for it is probably the most popular song amongst the Indians of the Andes. The 'band' warmed up too much, however, and a couple of harp-strings snapped, putting an end to the recital. They invited us to join them later in the month for their footfall fiesta, and then we set off on the long walk back to base camp.

On the outskirts of the village we were stopped by shouts and whistles from two Indian boys chasing after us along the path. We thought that perhaps one of us had dropped something, and waited for them to catch us up. But no! all they wanted was to walk with us to the next village. When we reached that village we were spread out, and as I walked through on my own, a pack of dogs set on me. One little one, braver than the others, took me by surprise and jumped up, knocking my glasses off with his paws. After that I always carried a handful of stones when we passed houses.

Pete Bebbington developed some bad blisters, and Vic and I waited while he doctored them. Pete Farrell was by now miles ahead, keeping up a remarkable pace. By the time we reached the farm, three hours after leaving Queropalca, we were completely parched; Pete Bebbington and I were even having difficulty in swallowing, owing to mucus in our throats. We passed some comments on the farmer's judgement of distances, and gratefully accepted some cognac from him. He introduced us to his family and lent us some Spanish *Reader's Digests*. After hearing the latest news about the Christine Keeler case we then pushed on to the base camp. It was dark by the time we reached the lake. Pete Farrell was putting up a fast pace and I was determined to keep up with him, although I was so tired and cold that I didn't care if I put my feet into bog or water. We were all looking forward to a hot meal and drinks when we got back. For the last two miles the only vision in my mind had been of a jam-jar full of steaming hot Ovaltine.

As I gruelled up the last steep slope into base camp I was convinced that I could smell stew, and sure enough Pete Westnidge, Dave Condict, Graham, and Charlie were sitting in the kitchen tent eating stew. Pete Farrell opened the stewpot and to our horror it was empty. The others had prepared only their own meal, leaving us to prepare ours when we arrived back. And there wasn't even any water in the bucket to make a drink with. The atmosphere could have been cut with a knife. Nobody spoke as the four of us, tired and hungry, prepared our meal. The other four sat in silence until they had finished their stew, when one by one they drifted back to their tents, taking their drinks with them.

Despite the fact that I was completely worn out after the day's route March I had difficulty in sleeping; and after midnight I went out for a walk down to the lake. It was a beautiful moonlit night, so bright that the lamp I took was not necessary. When I walked back up to the tents the camp was still and silent, except for talk and laughter coming from Dave Condict and Pete Westnidge. They were having one of their middle-of-the-night smokes and drinks.

I was sharing with Pete Bebbington his definitely one-man tent. As I went through a contortionist act to get into my sleeping-bag I inadvertently woke Pete up. He growled some pleasantry or other and turned over. Suddenly he shot upright as the sound of an enormous avalanche resounded round the valley. After that the night was a succession of disturbances, with Pete talking in his sleep, and me waking him with squeaks from the airbeds as I turned over. We were both glad when the morning came and we could get up.

We were supposed to be starting out for Rondoy that day, but nobody took the initiative and we spent the day sun-bathing and taking photographs. In the afternoon we made up the packs for the following day's climb up to the ice-basin. We knew that this would have to be the last of our attempts on Rondoy. There was a certain tension in the air, and nobody spoke much during the day.

Later, when we were settling down in our sleeping-bags for the night, Pete Bebbington told me his plans for the third and last attempt. He reckoned that the key to the ridge lay in making the ice-cave into a comfortable high camp, so that the assault party would be fresh when they started out along the ridge. This would mean moving airbeds, sleeping-bags, and extra supplies up from the ice-basin camp. And as the assault party (Pete Farrell and Vic, Pete Bebbington and Graham) would be loaded up with climbing gear, Dave Condict, Charlie, and myself were to act as support party, climbing up to the ice-cave with the extra supplies. While the assault party were out on the ridge we would wait in the ice-cave. If the ridge could be climbed without any major difficulty, Pete Bebbington would, when they returned to the ice-cave, go back up to the summit with me on his rope, while Charlie and Dave Condict would follow as a second rope. I doubted if this last part of the plan would be possible, but agreed to the logic of the rest of it. It seemed a good plan, even if it should be frustrating for those of us who were to be left in the ice-cave. It must be remembered that those of us who had not been on the ridge on the first attempt, had only Pete's judgement of the situation, as none of the other three had given us their views on the plan.

7

The Third Attempt: Base Camp to Ridge

Sunday, August 4th found us breakfasting early, for a change. It was a windy morning, though the sky was completely clear. Over breakfast, Pete Bebbington outlined his plans again for the benefit of the whole party. In the discussion that followed, Charlie objected to the three of us—Dave Condict, himself, and me—having to wait in the ice-cave during the three days that the ridge climb was expected to take. Nor did he think that we could reasonably expect Pete Bebbington to make—for our sakes—the climb from the ice-cave to the summit twice in a week. Pete explained that, in his opinion, four would be enough on the unknown but obviously dangerous ridge. He added, however, that if Charlie and Dave Condict wished to make the ridge climb as a third rope, on their own initiative and at their own risk, then nobody would object. But he made it clearly understood that the main efforts must be directed to supporting the original party of four. Charlie and Dave decided to have a go at it. As this meant that I should be left alone in the ice-cave for upwards of three days, Pete Bebbington volunteered that, if conditions permitted, I should join Graham and himself on the assault, climbing as a rope of three.

When all the details had been settled, we set off individually as soon as we were ready. I left first, picking my path up the moraine. Half an hour later, as I carefully wove my way in and out of the loose boulders that crowned it, I noticed that Vic—almost level with me—was taking the parallel route up the river valley, and was obviously finding it easier than mine. Vic and I arrived at the top of the moraine more or less at the same time; but as I had to repack my sack, which had been giving trouble, he went on up ahead of me. As I crossed the second scree slope I saw Pete Bebbington, Pete Farrell, and Charlie at the bottom of it, resting. I assumed that they were waiting for Graham and Dave Condict, who had just appeared at the top of the moraine. I continued on to the gully. I wanted to climb the strenuous haul up the grass gully while I was fresh. Vic by now had disappeared. At the top of the gully I sat down to wait for the others, as I was none too sure of the route.

Presently, the two Petes and Charlie arrived, and after a short rest we started off again. Graham and Dave Condict were still not in sight. The four of us climbed together up the steep slopes of *puna* grass and scree, onto the small snowfield below the rock-wall. In one of the chimneys on the rock route up the wall I caught my ice-axe in a crack. I was delicately perched with a foot on either side of the chimney, and the pick of the axe caught in an overhanging block. It took an awful lot of sweat and swearing to free the axe, and by the time I emerged at the top of the chimney the other three had disappeared. I continued on up to the first cairn on the ridge, but still nobody was in sight. As the route was obvious from this point, I decided to have something to eat while waiting for Graham and Dave Condict. Almost as soon as I sat down the sun disappeared behind Ninashanca, and with it the warmth of the day. As I pulled on a sweater I heard a shout. Since nobody was in sight I wondered who it could be and where the voice came from. I later discovered that it was Pete Farrell at the top of the abseil onto the glacier. He had shouted down to Pete Bebbington who was below, and in the direct line of a fall of ice that was tumbling down Rondoy Chico. Pete Bebbington glanced over his shoulder, saw the ice, leapt across the crevasse onto the glacier and went on running. The ice smashed onto the very spot where he had been standing. He had had a lucky escape.

The Third Attempt: Base Camp to Ridge

Unaware of what had happened I gave up waiting in the cold, and began to traverse round the ridge to the second cairn and first abseil. As I had had some difficulty on this abseil the first time, when the rope had caught on my rucksack, I now climbed down using the rope as a fixed rope. I followed the fresh tracks across the slopes of wet grit and snow that filled the gullies, and climbed up the opposite wall back onto the traverse line. After the first 100 feet of delicate traversing along the narrow ledge, I was relieved to come to the fixed ropes. These ended on the ledge at the top of the abseil rope leading into the basin. From there I could see that the first three men were already in the basin; two were almost at the tents, and the third (Charlie) half way across, picking his way through the avalanche debris. I decided again not to abseil, but twisted the rope round my arm and climbed down. The ice in the crevasse was hard and I couldn't find any tracks, so I stopped to put on my crampons and picked my own way through the séracs and across the two crevasses onto the glacier.

Although it was cold, the surface layer of snow on the glacier was soft, making it an arduous slog up to the tents. When I arrived everyone was changing into long-johns and Duvets. From the tents we could see the point of entry into the basin, and soon Graham and Dave Condict appeared. By the time they had crossed the basin a hot drink was waiting for them and the meal was well under way. Dave Condict had been slowed down by his breathing, which had been giving him some trouble and had made it necessary to stop frequently. He was to be hampered by this breathlessness for the whole of the climb on Rondoy.

While the meal was being prepared Dave Condict and I put up the extra tent. First we had to cut out a platform in the ice, as the other two tents had been pitched on the only level part of the platform. But as they had, with use, melted a groove nine or more inches deep, our tent was in fact on the only level spot. When we had finished, the meal was ready and we sat at the edge of the platform gazing out across the basin to the now moonlit hills in the distance. It was a beautiful clear and calm night, with the finishing touch added by the full moon as it edged its way round the ridge of Rondoy Chico to shine directly into the basin. We looked up at the face we were to climb in the early hours of the morning. It glowed in the bright moonlight, and we could make out every detail of the route we were to follow.

After the meal we sorted out the gear into loads, to be packed later, while someone began to melt ice for a drink. I retired to my sleeping-bag as soon as possible to continue reading *War and Peace*. Confronted by the problem of having no tin for the candle, I solved it by tying the candle to the tent-pole with a spare shoe-lace. Dave Condict came in ten minutes later with the drinks. It was a tiny tent, and he waited while I moved over; but in doing so I knocked the tent-pole out of place. Leaning over on one elbow I grasped the pole tightly to straighten it, and immediately let out a yell. It was almost red-hot where the candle had heated it! After this incident we had a smoke before settling down for four hours' sleep before the alarm went off at midnight; for as 'support party', Dave and I were to get up earlier than the rest, to make the breakfast.

At twelve the alarm duly woke us. Our tent was so small that only one of us could move at a time. Dave was awake first, and he slowly edged himself out of his sleeping-bag into the cold air, suitably lubricating the process with relevant curses. Dressing simply involved putting on boots and crampons, for we had slept fully clothed. Even this, however, seemed to be an effort, judging by Dave's language. As soon as he had crawled out of the tent I went through the same rigmarole. The main difficulty was to get into my boots, which had frozen and were stiff and contracted. The fact that my feet had swollen in the warm sleeping-bag did not make things easier. Outside, the air was cold and fresh, misty with suspended frost. The weather was ominous. A cloud-bank had appeared which completely covered the peaks and ridge of Rondoy, and came half way down the face. In the distance we

30. Leaving the ice-cave en route for the north summit

31. At the point where the pitch up from the ice-cave met the
beginning of the route along the ridge. The Cordillera Blanca
can be seen in the distance

could see three enormous orange balls of fire, from which shot frequent streaks of lightning to the invisible Amazon jungle. It was an impressive sight, and we stood watching it for a while before starting to prepare the breakfast.

Dave began to coax the stove into life while I collected and cleaned the bowls and jam-jars. It was a tricky operation, for the ice was so hard and slippery that to put anything down was to watch it slip down the slope and come to rest against the tent wall. As the ice was melting on the stove we sat watching the distant storm. Suddenly we had our own ball of fire! We heard a roar, and simultaneously the camp site was lit up as our tent burst into flames. I rushed across and—pulling on my leather gloves—hurriedly dragged out the contents of the tent. Our airbeds emerged as lumps of molten rubber, still burning. The rucksacks and sleeping-bags, being near the door, escaped almost undamaged. As I shovelled on snow to put out the fire, I looked for the cause and saw that the candle had burned down and set light to the groundsheet. The tent collapsed, looking rather sad.

I cleared up the mess as best I could while Dave Condict prepared the porridge. The others had been wakened by the noise of the fire, and we passed their breakfasts in to them. When we had eaten we put more ice on the stove for a drink and then began to pack. By now the others were emerging from their tents, and we sorted out the remainder of the loads. It seemed a long time before we had distributed the bits and pieces, Dave Condict and I being left with such awkward items as pressure cooker and biscuit-tin. At three o'clock Pete Farrell and Vic roped up, switched on their head-lamps and left the camp site. The rest of us followed a quarter of an hour later. Pete Bebbington, Graham and I were on one rope, with Dave Condict and Charlie bringing up the rear.

The route out of camp towards the ice-cave lay along the platform for 200 yards before it began to zig-zag its way up through the avalanche debris that provided bridges across the series of small crevasses. As we left the camp we could see the lamps of Vic and Pete Farrell as they moved backwards and forwards through this section. When we ourselves reached it and began to gain height, we had to stop every few yards because Charlie had no lamp and we had to pick out and light the path for him. The crampon marks of the first rope led out of this broken section onto a smooth ramp. (For details of the route, see Plates 18 and 19.) Dave Condict and Charlie came over the top of the ramp to join us, and the five of us went off along the platform together. After 100 yards the slope increased again as we climbed up a bulge directly below a small bergschrund. The route round the bergschrund lay up a ten-foot section on the rock-face.

The rock-pitch would have been tricky under any conditions; but with a heavy pack, wearing crampons, and with an ice-axe dangling from a karabiner at my waist, I was even more apprehensive. Graham led off up the pitch, stepping first onto the crest of a little ice-ridge that ran three feet from the rock. After some thought he leant across the gap between ice and rock, and placed his right foot up against the rock on a tiny flake ledge. Standing astride the gap, he felt round for a handhold and found nothing. He pulled his outstretched foot back and moved round to his left, repeating the same process. Then he moved back to the right, and this time managed to find a tiny handhold which enabled him to lever himself upright. Delicately he traversed back to his left, cursing his ice-axe. A firm foothold lifted him up to a good stance from which he could mantelshelf onto the top of the rock: three easy moves and he was over the bergschrund. I followed after him, trying desperately to remember his moves, helped by Pete who shone his torch for me. I too had trouble with my ice-axe, and hung on while I transferred it to a better position. A few curses, a bit of sweating, and I joined Graham, followed after a few minutes by Pete Bebbington. We waited for a while as Pete shone his lamp down for Charlie, and then started up a long gully.

The gully ran for about 800 feet at an angle of fifty-five degrees.

The climbing was strenuous, but not difficult. Snow pendants, formed by wind and sun, filled the gully and were a great help. We climbed together at a reasonably good speed, moving back onto the rock whenever one of us called for a rest. As we climbed this section, dawn broke. It was so impressive that we stopped for a while to watch it. There were no reds or pinks, only delicate gold and silver. The valleys below us were filled with clouds, which added to the impressiveness of the scene. (See Plate 16.) With the approach of day the clouds above us began to disappear and the ridge came into view, though we still could not see Vic or Pete Farrell. Charlie and Dave Condict were directly below us in the gully, moving slowly, Dave having difficulty with his breathing.

We continued on up the gully, which provided nothing worse than a hard slog. At the top of the gully we traversed out onto the face proper, moving up in a straight line towards the overhang that marks both the mid-point of the face and the half-way point of the day's climbing. We reached it at seven-thirty, just in time to see Vic and Pete Farrell leave. The slope directly beneath it increased to more than sixty-five degrees and called for considerable effort up the last 100 feet.

At the overhang we settled down for a long rest, waiting for Charlie and Dave Condict to arrive. The platform under the overhang was some thirty feet long, sloping in for ten feet. We sat smoking and eating, admiring the view, above all just glad to have our sacks off and be resting. An hour after we arrived Charlie came over the soft snow at the edge of the platform, followed by Dave Condict (see Plate 24).

Soon after they arrived Graham led off, stumbling thigh-deep through the soft snow at the edge of the platform and back onto the face. I followed, belaying when I reached him, and brought Pete to me while Graham continued on up. The route from the overhang followed the steps cut by Pete Farrell and Vic on the previous ascents, and at first went directly up, zig-zagging to gain height. The zig-zag stretch was up a seventy-degree slope and called for a rest every ten or so steps. To give maximum security we climbed caterpillar fashion: Graham would lead and find a belay position at the end of his rope, which gave him a 140-feet run-out. He would belay by thrusting his ice-axe into the hard snow, up to the pick, and running the rope round it. Then he would take a tension stance with the rope running round his waist, and call me up. I would climb up to him and take over his position, substituting my axe for his. Next Graham would lead off again and find another belay position, shouting down to me when he was secure. I would then bring Pete Bebbington up to me and he would take over my position while I climbed up to Graham, and then we would repeat the sequence. The disadvantage of this method is that each climber must remain still while *two* others climb a pitch. This was not too bad in the warm sunshine which we were enjoying on this occasion, but in cold weather it can be a trial, as it was to be later on this day. Even so, one's feet grew cold standing still on the steep snow; and, whenever we could, Pete and I would move on together while Graham belayed us both.

After we had gained 200 feet by zig-zagging, we traversed across to a rib of hard snow. In the gully which followed we climbed directly up again to gain height before traversing out onto the next rib and over it. We moved across a succession of ribs and gullies in this manner, gaining height in the gullies and traversing across the ribs. The last rib led us onto a traverse line leading directly to the foot of a triangular-shaped rock gully. Half way between the snow-rib and the rock gully was a rock stance: Graham led across to this, where I joined him. As the stance was too small for three, Graham led off again to a ledge at the bottom of the rock gully and belayed there, while I brought Pete round to me.

When Pete was belayed I moved across to Graham, carefully putting my feet in the steps that Vic had cut. The traverse was directly beneath an ice-overhang which accentuated the already impressive exposure. The face fell away from this point 3,000 feet to the ice-fall at the entrance to the ice-basin. As I reached Graham I noticed that there was little room on the rock-ledge on which he was belayed and asked him where he wanted me to stand. He told me to move below him into a small ice-hollow. I stretched across the gully and placed my right foot firmly on the ice, testing it for strength as it looked suspicious. Then, as it seemed all right, I moved the rest of my body across to it. Or at least I began to—for as soon as it took the full strain of my weight it gave way. Graham held me on a tight rope, as the ice platform plummeted down to the ice-fall. The rope ran across my left shoulder and I felt as if I had broken a bone. Four months later I discovered that I had in fact broken my scapula and damaged my shoulder nerves irreparably. But as I was hanging almost upside down, with the heavy pack keeping me overbalanced, my immediate problem was to get myself into an upright position. Graham and Pete watched, completely unable to help me. As Graham took the strain on the rope I found a hold for my left hand in the ice behind me and, lifting myself as high on it as possible, swung my ice-axe as high and as hard as I could. It held quite secure and I swung my left arm up and grasped the adze as hard as I was able; then, with a mantelshelf movement, brought my shoulders up to the level of my feet. Then I slowly cramponed down the side of the gully until I was standing with my face to the ice, from which position I could cut steps back up to join Graham on his ledge. Pete climbed across to us, and we decided to take a rest to settle our nerves and regain our strength.

It was an hour and a half before Charlie appeared over the last of the snow-ribs and began to traverse. We spent the time eating our remaining chocolate and talking of all the 'near things' we had experienced on earlier occasions. When Charlie appeared over the last rib, Pete decided to climb ahead up the rock gully and put up a fixed rope down to the rock-ledge. As he climbed up, rocks of all sizes began to shower down on Graham and me. We pressed ourselves to the rock, holding a rucksack over our heads to give extra protection, and watched the rocks bounce down to the glacier 2,500 feet below. I was glad that Graham had had a good belay.

Charlie meanwhile had reached the rock stance forty feet from us and was bringing Dave Condict round to join him there. We heard a shout from Pete and saw that he was ready to throw down the fixed rope, and was warning us to watch out for more falling stones. We pressed ourselves to the rock, none too soon, for as we did so a rock whistled past the place where we had been leaning, and embedded itself in the ice at our feet. The rope had snagged and fallen short of the ledge; so when Charlie and Dave were safely on the ledge out of the way of falling rocks, Graham climbed up free. He unravelled the rope and climbed down with it to another ledge ten feet above the one on which we were be-layed. Then he shouted to warn us that he was about to climb up to join Pete Bebbington, and would shout again when he reached the top. It seemed ages before we heard that shout. As soon as we did, I left the belay ledge and started climbing up the rock. The first thirty feet was up a succession of mantelshelf moves, which gradually forced me over to the right and onto the rotten ice in the gully. I climbed for ten feet or so up the ice and then traversed back onto the rock. Here I saw where the loose rock had been coming from, for the last 100 feet of the rock-rib was completely broken, and littered with rocks of all sizes. It would have been difficult not to have knocked any down even without crampons; but with them on, it was impossible not to send a shower down with every few moves.

As I started up this last section a bitterly cold wind suddenly began to blow down from the ridge, bringing with it thick, swirl-ing mist. Frozen through, I climbed as quickly as I could. Pete and Graham above me, and Charlie and Dave Condict below me, had disappeared in the cloud. I was surprised, when I did arrive at the top, to see through the mist Pete and Graham crouched only a few feet away from me. The rope ran to a piton fixed into the ice above Graham's head. As the only two 'seats' available were occupied, I had to stand with my pack balanced on the ice and steady myself with a finger in a piton.

It was intensely cold, and as we waited we cheered ourselves by cursing Charlie who seemed to be taking longer than anyone. We could not climb on, as it was our rope that Charlie and Dave Condict were using as a fixed rope. When Charlie did appear we all had a cursing match—Charlie cursing us for kicking stones down on him, and we cursing Charlie for taking so long. In fact the cold was making us all inconsiderate.

Graham led off on the next pitch, using Charlie's rope, while Charlie brought Dave Condict up, now using the fixed rope as a top rope. Another fixed rope led from the piton along the next part of the route. Graham climbed up to the piton and moved along and round a corner out of sight. It was a short pitch, and soon I heard Graham calling me to follow him. I was glad to be moving again, but it was not for long. I traversed along on the narrow ledge, using the fixed rope for twenty feet until I found Graham on his belay. (This belay point was that of the rear climber in Plate 28, taken when the route was being pioneered, which explains the absence of a fixed rope.) I took over his belay onto a piton and he in turn moved on. The next pitch was across a steep patch of hard ice, breaking at the far side into chaotic formations, and completely overhung by a wall of rotten ice with icicles hanging from it. Half way across, the route climbed up to another piton in which Graham put a running belay as added protection to the fixed rope. From there a succession of awkward moves led across the broken ice and up to a saddle point in the next ice-rib. Graham very delicately picked his way through the broken ice, eventually reaching the saddle ledge and yelling back to me to bring round Pete Bebbington.

Pete moved quickly over the easy section up to my stance,

which he took over from me. At first, as I climbed towards Graham, it was only a question of using the steps cut in the ice, miniature holds that I hardly believed would hold me. The sense of exposure on this section was very great, and I was unspeakably grateful for the fixed rope. I calculated that, with a 50 lb pack, I weighed in all close on two hundredweight: this, I decided, was a ridiculous weight with which to tempt the little ice formations that the route led onto. It was fortunate that, as I watched my feet find each hold, the mist blocked out the view between my legs. It seemed ages before I joined Graham; it probably was. His stance was too small for the two of us, so he moved on a little before I took it over.

The next pitch was the artificial one that Vic had engineered across the ice-gully. Graham held onto the first sling and karabiner and leant forward to reach hold of the second. When he reached it, he put all his weight onto the second, and swung across to the thin ice-ledge, grasping hold of the fixed rope as he moved. His feet landed on the ledge and he relaxed. As soon as he did so the ice formation gave way, shattering down the gully. Graham hung onto the fixed rope and moved quickly across the last few feet and onto a saddle in the opposite rib. He stood there resting against the ice for a few minutes. Pete Bebbington had heard the ice breaking and shouted round to ask what was happening. I shouted back that everything was fine and that he could be getting ready to come round. Meanwhile Graham, having recovered from the shock, moved up the gully he was now in, to reach a piton where he belayed.

I brought Pete up to me and we again went through the process of changing over the belay. I pushed in my ice-axe and moved down into the gully, Pete climbed up onto the saddle and took over the piton. Despite the fact that I knew I had a top rope, a rear rope, and a fixed rope, and that both Pete and Graham were securely anchored to pitons, I was still a little apprehensive about the move, after seeing the ice break away under Graham. While

Pete encouraged me with pleasant comments about wasting time, I swung across. It turned out to be easy for me; for as I was much taller than Graham, my swing took me to the far side of the ledge, which was much thicker and stronger than the section that had collapsed.

Graham shouted down to me to stay where I was. We were now at the foot of the final seventy-foot gully leading up to the ice-cave. The next pitch led right up to the cave, with no reasonable stance on the way. This presented a problem. We were climbing on a 120-foot rope which gave us about fifty-five feet between us, allowing for the rope tied round our waists. This would mean that Graham would be pulled up fifteen feet short of the ice-cave amongst the overhanging, rotten ice. He suggested that I untie from our rope, move up, and belay to the piton while he climbed the last pitch. I wasn't too pleased with the plan, but there was nothing else for it. I shouted back to Pete telling him what we were doing and climbed up to Graham. He untied himself from the piton and moved up. I tried to clip a karabiner into the piton but failed, as the karabiner was a large Stubai type and would not fit through the hole. The only way I could belay was by putting the index finger of my left hand through the piton and holding tight. I chopped away some more ice from the foot stance, making it big enough for the whole of my left boot, which made me feel a bit safer.

While I was hacking away at the solid ice we heard a shout from above. We looked up and could see, blurred by the mist, a head covered with fur. I thought at first that the tales we had been told in Chiquian of the Old Woman of the Mountains who was supposed to live on Rondoy, were true after all. I was surprised to hear that she spoke good English, albeit with a broad Manchester accent. It was Pete Farrell looking out of the ice-cave. He had heard the ice-axe and was shouting down to ask if Graham wanted a top rope. This seemed a very good idea. Graham caught the end of the rope that Pete Farrell threw down, and tied onto it. By now, muffled groans could be heard from the other three. They could neither see nor hear us and had no idea of what was going on.

Graham started climbing and soon disappeared into the mist. I began to appreciate, by its absence, the psychological help of being tied onto a rope. I watched the rope as it paid out between Graham and Pete Bebbington, realizing more intensely than ever that the only things between me and the glacier below were my cramped finger through the piton and a boot cramponed firmly into the ice. Particles of ice were showering down on me as Graham climbed, and I pulled my cagoul hood over my neck. It seemed ages before the ice-shower stopped. As soon as Graham was in the ice-cave Pete Farrell shouted down to warn me that he was throwing the top rope down again. It was a good throw, coming within a few inches of me. As I tied onto it I felt infinitely safer.

Graham also gave me some slack on the rope from him to Pete Bebbington; I tied back onto this as well, and shouted down to Pete, telling him to climb. A yell came back and the rope slackened as he untied his belay. I only had the slackness of the rope as a gauge to how fast Pete was climbing. A sudden increase in the rate of slackening told me that he had swung across the gully, and I took the slack in quickly. Pete suddenly yelled: 'Take in.' The rope was already tight, but he yelled again: 'Take in slack.' I saw that the rope had caught on an ice-knob, and climbed down a few feet as quickly as I could, shouting down to Pete to tell him what I was doing. With a sweep of my ice-axe I chopped off the offending knob of ice and climbed back up again, taking in the slack as I went. I shouted down to Pete that he could climb again, and in a few seconds he appeared at the bottom of the gully ten feet below me.

He rested on the saddle ledge while I untied from the top rope. I climbed up a few feet until I found a comfortable perch, and Pete climbed up to the piton and belayed. I remained tied onto the rope between Graham and Pete Bebbington, and used the top rope Pete Farrell had thrown down as a fixed rope. When I shouted up to Pete Farrell that I was starting to climb, he took the rope in until it was very tight: too tight in fact. But when I shouted 'slack' he thought I meant 'take in slack', and pulled the rope so tight that it was difficult for me to breathe. The gully was near vertical, composed of very hard ice, into which it was impossible to bite the crampons. The ice-axe too was useless on the hard ice, and I pushed it through my waist length, where—as it caught in my overboots as I climbed—it was more of a liability than an asset.

On the more open stretches, Vic had hacked steps out of the ice which were a great help. But for the rest it was a question of finding your own holds in the broken ice. After thirty feet the gully was split in two by a rib of rotten ice running down the middle. The steps led up the right-hand sub-gully, at first away from the ice-cave. As I climbed up, the ropes became twisted over the rib, and as Pete Farrell took in the rope to me he also took in the fixed rope which I was using for balance. I shouted up to him, and as he was sorting out the ropes, one of them caught on the ice. I leant up to free it, putting all my weight on a handhold in the rotten ice. The hold came away and I spun backwards off my footholds. Pete Farrell held me on a tight rope as I righted myself. Swinging round I lifted my left foot back up to its hold; but in so doing caught my ice-axe in my overboot, so that the axe shot up and knocked open my camera case. I instinctively grabbed for the camera, which fell out, and in doing so I fell back into the gully. My feelings were running high by now and I was cursing everything in sight. To steady myself, I hammered in the heel points of my crampons and rested for a while. Pete Bebbington below was yelling up to ask me what the hell I was doing. 'Trying out some new dance steps,' I replied, and climbed back onto the rib, this time successfully. A few easy moves up the rib led into the left-hand sub-gully. The last five feet were vertical but well supplied with footholds. At the top I loomed up to find myself face to face with Pete Farrell, a few feet away in the ice-cave. I clambered through the entrance and into the cave, grateful to be there after ten and a half hours on the face. Pete and Vic had been there since nine o'clock, taking only six hours for the 3,000-foot climb up the face from the basin to the ridge. Later they were to break even this record.

When I had untied from the rope, Pete Farrell shouted down to Pete Bebbington that he could now climb up. It was good to take my pack off for the last time that day, and I quickly opened it to take out my Duvet. I had been longing for its warmth since the clouds had come down and enveloped us with cold. Vic came in through the entrance on the other side to the one I had used, and gave me a jam-jar of steaming hot orangeade. I wrapped my hands round the jar and sipped the drink. Looking round the cave I was surprised to find how accommodating it was. Vic said that, since they arrived, Pete Farrell and he had been raising the roof with their ice-axes and filling in some of the hollows in the floor. It would be difficult to imagine a more convenient ice-cave, complete with shelves and draught-excluders. Vic had converted the veranda into a kitchen where he was beginning to prepare the evening meal, and he was constantly melting ice to provide us each with a warm drink as we arrived.

When Pete Bebbington came through the entrance it was obvious that seven of us would not be able to move freely about the cave. Graham and I pulled our sleeping-bags on and went to the far end of the cave to be out of the way. Pete Bebbington went out onto the veranda to help Vic with the meal. Graham and I sat talking about the route while Pete Farrell continued to bring people up the last gully. It was more than an hour later that Charlie and Dave Condict appeared. They had been slowed down on the traverse section by Dave's having to remove and coil the fixed rope as he climbed—an operation presenting some problems, especially when crossing the artificial pitch. By the time they had both arrived in the ice-cave they had spent four and a half hours on the last 400 feet.

The pressure stove lid had broken on the way up and we were going to have a long wait before the dehydrated meal was ready. As soon as Dave Condict appeared, we took the biscuit-tin from the top of his pack. After we had each taken about three biscuits Charlie sat on the tin, murmuring something about high-altitude emergency rations. Someone else murmured something entirely different, whereupon the biscuit-tin appeared again and stayed open until nothing was left but a collection of mixed crumbs at the bottom.

It was dark well before the meal was ready. But meanwhile Pete Bebbington had cut holders in the ice for candles, and the reflection of the candlelight on the ice walls and roof gave us good illumination. I wondered what any Indian, chancing to look up and see the yellow glow on the ridge, would think of it. I was confident that he would describe to later expeditions how he had seen lights in the home of the Old Woman of the Mountains. As we sat round talking and smoking in the now warm, candlelit cave, it was difficult to appreciate that we were 19,000 feet up Rondoy, and that six feet away on either side of us were steep faces sheering away over 3,000 feet to the glaciers below. It felt as though we were sitting around a camp site in Chamonix. We congratulated Vic and Pete Farrell on their route-finding, especially Vic on his route through the last ice-pitches, and on his luck in finding the cave.

Later, Pete Bebbington told me what I had already assumed when the weather turned—namely, that it would be ridiculous for a rope of three to climb along the ridge. This meant that I must, after all, stay alone in the ice-cave for two days, since Dave Condict and Charlie had definitely decided to go for the summit on their own initiative. I was disappointed, but it was obvious that a rope of three would have been difficult on the ridge even in good weather, and that in the prevailing cold wind, cloud, and threatened snow, it was quite out of the question.

The cave was cramped when the seven of us had stretched out in our sleeping-bags. Pete Bebbington and Vic were sleeping on the upper platform and the rest of us in the lower section. As the first person in, I eventually found myself wedged between Graham's Duvet and the ice wall, unable to move, with the roof a couple of inches over my head. I decided not to risk suffocation, and crawled over the other four onto the upper section. I also decided—when I took another look at the drop—against sleeping on the veranda, and so I slept in a sitting position wedged in a corner, half on the ice and half on my airbed, with Pete Bebbington's and Vic's feet on top of me. I didn't in fact sleep much, spending most of the night listening to Dave Condict, who was suffering from Cheyne-Stokes breathing. Apart from Dave's chronic breathing troubles, and the general breathlessness of us all, we had more or less escaped from altitude effects. Graham and Pete Farrell had grown enormous cold sores on their faces, and my gums were constantly bleeding, but nobody suffered from the usual *sorroche* bouts of nausea and headaches. Psychologically we seemed to be as normal as we could ever be, though nerves became easily frayed and patience quickly exhausted—and perhaps Charlie did seem a little more than ever worried about the future of the Welsh.

Vic was up at four in the morning and began the preparations for breakfast. Pete Bebbington soon joined him on the veranda. There was no movement from the others, who slept soundly until five-thirty when Vic came in with the breakfast of Weetabix and orangeade. The weather had worsened in the night, visibility was down to twenty feet and it was threatening to snow. It was depressing to see them go off: Pete Farrell and Vic first, closely followed by Pete Bebbington and Graham, with Charlie and Dave Condict half an hour later. I went out onto the veranda to watch Dave Condict traverse twenty feet across the face and disappear into the mist. Then I scoured out the breakfast pots with handfuls of snow and surveyed my solitary domain. I discovered that the petrol stove was not working and that the only gas stove refill I had been left was virtually empty. I also found that my gas cigarette-lighter had run out of fuel and that I had very few matches. Apart from tinned biscuits and jam, I had no food except dehydrated meals which would have required prolonged cooking. All in all I was not too well off.

I moved my airbed into a more comfortable position, pulled on my now soaking sleeping-bag, and fell off to sleep immediately. When I awoke at midday it was to find myself covered with a layer of powdered snow. Mist was swirling into the cave through both entrances, carrying with it more powdered snow. Snow was also pouring through the holes in the roof, sliding down from the ridge and into the cave. I struggled out of my sleeping-bag, shook the snow off it, and went to the doors. Visibility was down to a few feet, though suddenly a wind blew up, and for a moment I could see down to base camp before the mist closed in again. With an airbed and two ice-axes I erected a shelter over the part of the cave that I was using. I lit a cigarette and applied some thought to the match shortage. I calculated that, though I could not afford to use a match every time I wanted a cigarette, I was not short of candles. Therefore I could light a candle and use it to light my cigarettes. I then cross-calculated that to justify the waste of a candle, I should have to smoke a lot.

Everything organized, I settled down in my sleeping-bag to read *War and Peace*. The snow continued to pour through the holes in my makeshift shelter. I chewed some of it to quench my thirst and discovered that the fresh flakes, more like soft hail-stones, melted quite easily in the mouth. I mixed some orangeade powder with it and finished up with a pleasant thirst-quencher. Later in the afternoon the snow stopped, though the clouds remained quite low. I took advantage of the lull to use the last of the gas to cook some soup.

Meanwhile, down in base camp, Pete Westnidge too was whiling away his time by reading. Unlike me, he did have the occasional visitor. On the Monday, while he had been watching us climb the face, two Indian girls had visited him in an attempt to sell him some milk and potatoes. He had some language difficulties, especially when trying to explain that they could not have any of the empty paraffin cans, which we needed to help pay for the hire of mules. The following day the farmer visited him with news of the mules about which we had been enquiring. He had been able to arrange mules for us through another of his brothers, but could not find a horse for Pete. Pete was left wondering whether he could develop wings before we all moved to the other side of the range. Soon after the farmer left, it began to hail down in the base camp too, making Pete wonder how all of us on Rondoy were getting on. Not knowing of the re-arranged plan, he had expected Dave Condict, Charlie, and me to come down the face again that day.

That night, of Tuesday, August 6th, I was awakened in the ice-cave by what I took to be an earth tremor. Later when I asked Charlie if they had felt anything on the ridge he told me that they hadn't. So I put it down to vibrations of my airbed. Weeks later I read in a Lima newspaper of how I had been to a press conference where I had related with great emotion 'the tale of how I had spent the night alone at 19,000 feet in the ice-cave with an earthquake shattering the ridge and sending down huge avalanches on all sides' (*sic!*). The newspaper report was the first I had heard of my press conference.

32. Jirishanca from the north summit of Rondoy

33. Yerupaja, with Yerupaja Chico on its left

8

Rondoy

When the summit party left the ice-cave on the Tuesday, they had gone out into a cold and cloudy morning. The cloud was drifting low round the ridge, and it was rarely possible to see beyond the full run-out of the rope. This was no great problem for the first two ropes—Pete Farrell and Vic, Pete Bebbington and Graham—for they had already been over the route when they had climbed the north summit nine days earlier. But for Charlie and Dave Condict, who did not know the way, it presented more of a difficulty; for they had to follow, as best they could, the route that the others had taken. The poor visibility reduced them to following the footsteps in the snow and on the ice, and where possible taking bearings from pitons and fixed ropes.

The summit climb was expected to take two days, so that when they left the cave the six members of the summit parties were carrying packs weighed down with enough food and equipment for two bivouacs. There was no warming-up period as there had been the day before on the face climb. From the cave the route lay straight onto the almost vertical ice of the west face. A few steps down off the veranda led to an awkward traverse up to the right, which avoided a heavily icicled bulge of loose ice. (See Plate 30 of Pete Farrell on this section.) As Dave Condict climbed out of the cave he was very conscious that on the nearly vertical ice of the day before, in the gully below the cave, he had had both a top rope and a fixed rope, with a good belay for the leader. Now the rope, pulled taut, disappeared into the eddying greyness that was both above and below him. He gingerly climbed up a steep ice-rib to Charlie who was belayed thirty feet up on the ridge. From this point the ridge curved away steeply to the right. They climbed up it, following the marks made by the earlier parties, who had by now completely disappeared into the mist.

A full run-out took Charlie and Dave along the smooth cornice that formed the ridge, and to the foot of a wall of rotten ice. The snow on the ridge was soft and powdery and Dave was slowed down by his poor breathing. From the wall it was necessary to flounder for twenty feet, down a steep snow-gully leading onto the firmer snow of the ramp which lay immediately below the north summit and underneath a huge towering overhang. They followed the steps which led them onto a traverse down to the left. At the end of the traverse they caught up with the first two ropes who were still on the severe pitch leading to the north summit.

While they were waiting for the next pitch to be cleared, Dave used the time trying to free a piton, which was no longer needed there, but might have proved useful further along the ridge. Despite all his efforts the piton refused to budge, and it remains as one of the many items of equipment that we were forced to leave behind on Rondoy. The cloud was still thick and low, but by now the sun was up: and though it failed to break through the cloud, it warmed the air appreciably.

When Graham eventually shouted down that the pitch was clear, Charlie started climbing. The traversing line brought them up against a fifteen-foot-high ice-rib, which they climbed round, to be forced immediately into a hunched position under the over-hang. The ice at shoulder level had melted into flake-like forma-tions providing secure handholds, but there was little or nothing for the crampons to grip on. A delicate forty feet of traverse from this point brought them to a second, larger, ice-rib, onto which they climbed, finding a belay ledge on the rib itself.

Apart from his breathing, Dave was confronted with another problem. On the previous day he had found that a Dexion strapped horizontally to his pack had caught on the ice when traversing across the face. Now, having strapped it on in a vertical position, he found that it was catching on the overhang, thus preventing him from taking full advantage of the space available and from relaxing in comfort.

They waited on this platform until Graham shouted down again that the next pitch was clear. The route lay up the rib and into the cloud above them. The first step was awkward. It was high and delicate as Pete Farrell had previously found, and was followed by two or three paces across a fragile, almost transparent ice-roof onto a steep wall of highly polished ice, immediately to the right of the rib. The earlier parties had put up a fixed rope on this ice-wall, and at the top had hammered in two pitons as a secure belay. Charlie and Dave were grateful to find the rope when they approached the wall. Charlie climbed up first and found the wall pock-marked with convenient natural handholds melted by the sun into the ice.

A few feet above the belay the route led back onto the rib and continued up what appeared to be a very brittle cornice. The rib ran to the top of the ridge, its peak forming the north summit of Rondoy. When Charlie and Dave traversed off the rib to the left, the mist was so thick that they had no idea that they were passing under the north summit. The traverse line gained height and brought them onto the heavily corniced ridge that runs between the north and south summits. The ridge dropped away in a series of smooth, rounded 'bumps', curving off to the right. (See Plate 32 of Pete Farrell on the section.) It was not until they reached this point that Charlie and Dave Condict realized that they had passed the north summit.

On the second 'bump' they met with a mishap. Charlie had led off for about fifteen feet from Dave's belay when he was suddenly brought to an abrupt halt. The rope had snagged. It had caught on a piece of rock somewhere under the left side of the ridge, which at this point curved away smooth and regularly from the cornice, suddenly steepening six feet down, and in places overhanging the steep face below. Charlie and Dave both tugged hard at the rope, but it failed to come free. Jerks and flicks also failed. They had no spare rope with them and could not afford to leave this one, so they decided to try and pull it through. Dave untied and Charlie attempted to free it by coiling it in. The rope moved a little and then stuck fast again, this time refusing to move at all. Furious, Charlie climbed down and cut the rope, leaving them with fifty feet of the 120-foot full-weight nylon. More important, though, was the fact that it had cost them fifteen minutes.

The length of the rope restricted them to short run-outs, which slowed them down considerably. Given the broken nature of the ridge, this was in some ways an advantage; on the other hand, the forty-five-foot pitches often fell short of a good belay.

The smooth, regular undulations of the ridge began to change. The snow curved down at first, and then up a little to a short five-foot step-up of yellow and red rock, which was capped by a further eight feet or so of snow and ice. (See Plate 34.) The cornice was falling away from the rock ridge, and just as the move onto this bump had been awkward, so was the move off it. A delicate step was needed to avoid breaking through the cornice on the right, or falling off the ridge to the left. They stepped down onto the bare rock of the exposed ridge, which was loose and broken, their crampons scratching about looking for secure footholds. Two tottering steps across the rock and they were able to jam the ice-axes into the next ice-bump, a mushroom-shaped formation over ten feet high.

There was no way round the crumbling side of the mushroom. The only way over it was to push in their ice-axes at full reach, using them to steady their balance as they climbed precariously up. They moved up, as gently and smoothly as was possible, hoping that the creaks and groans that were coming from the ice did not mean that the whole formation was about to topple off the ridge. They went through the reverse of the process on the other side, to bring themselves back onto the ridge.

On the other side of the mushroom the ridge ran away for

fifty feet, a knife edge, never more than two feet wide. The sudden confrontation of this obstacle reminded Dave of the Chamonix Aiguilles; he had the same momentary sense of surprise and alarm as you get there when a strong pull-up brings you, not to the next hold, but almost over the top of the ridge itself. The rock, however, was not like Chamonix granite, but was insecure and liable to flake away. Further on, the ridge became smooth and faultless, falling away sharply on either side.

Charlie led along this section of the ridge as a tight-rope walker would have done, balancing with his arms outstretched. He belayed on a smooth ramp at the far end and called to Dave to follow him. At first Dave tried to traverse along one face of the ridge, using the crest of the ridge for handholds. The loose rock forced him to give up this method and he continued in a straddling position, as if he were playing leap-frog.

The clouds had cleared slightly and visibility improved. They could see a prominent rock-gendarme fifty feet away and beyond it a wide snow saddle (clearly visible in Plate 18), which sloped down from the crest of the ridge at a gentle angle for 250 feet, ending abruptly in an overhang. Below this again was a 3,000-foot drop onto the Oggione glacier.

The gendarme cut off the rest of the view with the same finality with which it had blocked the ridge and checked Pete Farrell on the second summit attempt. Dave balanced the fifty feet to the gendarme (see Plate 34) with his feet on the rock ridge and his hands resting on the top of the cornice which rose four to six feet vertically above its right-hand side. As he was climbing he saw that the first two parties were both at the foot of the gendarme where the cornice flattened out and disappeared, and the ridge broadened to form a comfortable platform.

On the platform the two earlier ropes had already spent some time trying to find a way up the gendarme. Immediately above and to the right of the platform the rock rose sheer and unbroken, giving no route at all. When Charlie and Dave arrived, Vic was adjusting his belay to allow Pete Farrell to move down a twelve-foot wall and traverse round twenty feet to the left of the gendarme, on steep sloping snow. From there, a crack ran to the top of the block. At the bottom the crack was extremely thin, but as it rose it widened into two distinct cracks, filled with broken rock.

Both Pete Farrell and Vic moved down and round to the bottom of the crack, belayed by Pete Bebbington. Pete Farrell took his crampons off and swung up into the first part of the crack, with Vic directly below him on the snow. By now the weather had turned again. The clouds hung thicker than ever, reducing visibility considerably, and conditions were worsened by a bitter wind and the first few flakes of a snowfall. Graham, Charlie, and Dave sat shivering on the platform waiting for their turns to climb. Where the cracks divided, Pete Farrell hesitated for a while before moving into the left one. After a few minutes Pete Farrell shouted down that he was belayed, when Vic began to climb. The rest followed without difficulty, but slowly; and it was three hours after he had first sat down before Dave Condict—last of all —began to climb.

No sooner had he realized that the first move into the crack was a loose hand-jam at full stretch, than he appreciated the slowness of the first five. He pulled his gloves off and, after jamming his right hand high in the crack, pulled up on his numb hands, at the same time strenuously swinging his body to the left off the sloping foothold and into the crack. With half his body jammed in the crack, he rested for a few minutes to recover his breath. His hands began to hurt as he held himself in position, and he quickly reached out full stretch again to grasp the top of a block, onto which he struggled. Charlie peered down anxiously from above as Dave carefully calculated his route up the last ten feet of 'moderate' climbing as though it were at least 'very severe'.

The top was heavily corniced and Dave was grateful to move beside Charlie into the belay which was screened from the now heavy snow and bitter cold wind. They stopped only to pull on their overboots and crampons before moving to the edge of the platform, where they found that Pete Farrell had fixed up an abseil rope which hung down into a shallow gully of loose rock and snow. Dave tied onto the 300-foot nylon rope which they had picked up from one of the other parties, and went down first, looking for the steps that the others must have made from the point where they had begun to traverse the snow saddle. The visibility was so poor, with the wind whipping the snow up into a white torment, that Dave abseiled past the traverse point without seeing it and had to climb the fifteen feet back up to the footsteps. By the time he was back, Charlie too had abseiled down the 100 feet, and they were able to set off immediately across the saddle. Pete Bebbington and Graham came into view for a short time, just two rope-lengths in front.

The snow was so soft and powdery that occasionally a step would give way, when an ice-axe would have to be thrust in quickly. Forty feet after starting Dave lost the footsteps of the parties in front and kicked out a new line. Charlie, coming up behind, was puzzled by this, for he could see that the new set of steps that Dave was kicking was precisely two feet above the steps of the first two ropes! The next two rope-lengths took them across firmer snow and ice to a rock-rib that ran up to the crest of the ridge. Beyond this, another rope-length brought them to a second rock-rib. By now it was nearly dark. Charlie climbed over the rib and to the full length of the rope, disappearing from sight. Dave shouted to ask if he should climb, and was answered with silence. After a while the rope jerked three times. Dave took this to be a signal to climb and, removing his ice-axe belay, traversed across to the rib. As soon as he had reached it, a shout came down from Charlie telling him to go back. He retraced his steps and took up his belay position again. The moment he did so another shout came from Charlie, this time telling him to climb. This time he reached the rib and crossed it into a very steep snow-gully running up alongside the rib into the cloud and what remained of daylight.

The rope ran directly up from Dave to Charlie, and although they were unable to see each other they could talk quite freely. Charlie shouted down to Dave telling him to find a bivouac site for the night. Dave shouted back up that there was not the remotest chance of his finding a bivouac site anywhere near where he was standing. He awaited a reply. None came. Night fell, enveloping him in blackness and biting cold. Lumps of ice began to rain down on him. In the moments of stillness he cursed up into the heavens, but there was no reaction. Nothing happened. He could see no movement, hear no shouts, and soon the ice-lumps began to pour down on him again.

At long last he heard Charlie's voice telling him to climb. Dave moved upwards in the direction of the voice. The snow in the gully was soft and crumbling; every step broke under him, making progress slow. After climbing for sixty feet he could hear more voices and the barrage of ice grew heavier. He suddenly found himself in the beams of three lamps; he had reached the others, or at least, Pete Bebbington, Graham, and Charlie. It was seven o'clock.

Graham and a couple of rucksacks were balanced on a ledge about three feet by two feet, on the left side of the gully. Three feet below him were Pete Bebbington and Charlie on a ledge about the same size, but which Pete was enlarging by hacking at the ice with his ice-axe. It was these enlargement operations, and those of Pete Farrell and Vic thirty feet higher, that had sent the ice down on Dave. He crossed onto the ledge where—when they had sorted out themselves and their rucksacks—he took his turn at hacking at the back of the small bergschrund to make a platform large enough for the four of them to spend the night on.

When he asked Pete Bebbington 'Where are we?', he received the reply: 'About fifty feet below the summit. Pete Farrell and Vic were there about five-thirty.'

Pete Farrell and Vic had apparently reached the gully a little before five, climbing through rotten ice at the top and emerging onto the south and highest summit of Rondoy. Pete Farrell later told us that Vic let out a victorious yell as he climbed on top of the summit ice-cap. Rondoy had been climbed for the first time ever. Our expedition had succeeded in its main purpose.

When Pete Farrell and Vic had reached the summit, it had been too dark to take photographs, and they are not the flag-waving type; so they had climbed down to a small crevasse which they noticed twenty feet below the summit. There they spent the night, with the others thirty feet below them.

It was not until midnight that these four managed to settle down. The exertion of cutting out the platform had warmed them up a little and also tired them. They were grateful for the soups that Graham had so patiently been cooking, balancing a mug over the gas stove which he held in his free hand, and using his head-torch to light up the ice for those engaged below in excavations. When they had enlarged the platform as much as possible, they inflated two airbeds and laid them along the ledge. Graham, Charlie, and Dave sat on the airbeds with their backs and shoulders against the back wall. Their feet hung well over the ledge into the gully, their only protection being a length of Dexion pushed into the snow at the edge of the platform. Pete Bebbington lay lengthways, his feet and legs across those of the others, with his head and shoulders in a little cave that he had hollowed out of the ice at the end of the bergschrund. Taking off their boots to prevent them freezing on their feet, and putting on Duvet socks, they managed to wriggle into their sleeping-bags. Dave was worried that he wasn't going to be able to sleep, but by twisting over onto his right side, he could rest his head on Charlie's chest where he was soon snoring away quite happily, much to the consternation of the others.

Almost as if by prearrangement all four of them awoke at four o'clock the next morning. It was a cold and grey morning; the Zarsky sack which they had drawn over themselves was thickly covered by snow that had fallen in the night. It had now stopped snowing, however, and they cooked breakfast. Charlie held the gas stove, while Dave and Pete Bebbington took turns at holding the mug over the flames. The mug was used for brewing everything, from chocolate and soup, to Marmite and jam. They followed this with tinned oatmeal biscuits and then tinned herrings, which they found were not improved by freezing before serving.

Graham was nearest to the sacks and crampons, and also to the end of the ledge giving the easier access to the gully. He was therefore the first to struggle into his boots and crampons, followed by Dave, Pete, and then Charlie. While they were preparing themselves for the day's climbing, Vic shouted down from above that he and Pete Farrell would remain where they were, until the other four had climbed above them. Meanwhile dawn had risen, brilliant on an almost colourless sky. The valleys were filled with fresh snow, and the low cloud seemed almost ready to evaporate. An endless series of photographs was taken, of the sunrise, of the bivouac site, and of each other. This involved complicated movements among the four of them on the already cramped ledge, where only one person could move at a time. Every movement had to be carefully calculated; a careless move by Graham sent his mug, a tin of sardines and a packet of soup-powder bouncing down into the gully and out of sight into the void below. He commented: 'We didn't want the soup anyway, did we?'

By the time they started climbing, the sun was high in the sky, and though cloud drifted idly across the snow far below, it was warm and bright. For almost the first time since they had left the ice-cave, they could see further than the length of the rope. Pete Bebbington led off up the gully, now of hard snow and ice, with a thin covering of fresh snow; Graham soon joined him. Charlie and Dave followed up to the bivouac site that Pete Farrell and Vic had by now vacated. Graham was belayed on the top of the ridge, fifteen feet above them. Ten feet above again, and to the right of Graham, was the insignificant-looking cornice that formed the summit.

As Dave and Charlie watched from below, Pete Bebbington

carefully balanced up to the top. A step gave way—the snow almost too powdery to hold his axe—but Pete pulled his way over and onto the summit. He took his pack off and, half squatting, took out his camera and waited for the cloud to clear.

Below him, as Graham waited, and Charlie and Dave settled in the crevasse, Pete Farrell and Vic disappeared from sight down the gully and onto the snow saddle. Eventually, Pete despaired of the cloud ever clearing and packed away his camera after taking several photographs of what view there was. As he pulled his rucksack back onto his shoulders, the cloud cleared. He carefully reversed the procedure, and immediately the clouds re-appeared. There was another long wait for those below. The same thing was repeated three times, until impatient noises from below began to break into Pete's solitary vigil on the summit and he climbed down. Dave and Charlie moved out of the crevasse and into the gully, stamping in their steps as Graham and Pete climbed down past them. Charlie quickly climbed up to the ridge, but time had been wasted. Pete Farrell and Vic were a good hour ahead of them on the way down, and Pete Bebbington and Graham were already at the bottom of the gully. On the basis of the previous ropes' experience they calculated that climbing to the summit would cost another thirty minutes. They decided that as two ropes had already been to the summit, the climb up the last triumphant steps would not justify the necessary time and effort.

Forgoing Charlie's ambition to fly the Welsh flag from the summit, they hammered in a length of Dexion, from which they abseiled 150 feet down the gully. Dave went first and arrived at the foot of the rock-rib just as Pete Bebbington began to move round it and onto the snow saddle. They exchanged greetings. Dave was unable to find a secure belay and Charlie had to stop ten feet above him. They pulled in the rope, losing time because they had to coil it again into the 150-feet double length. Charlie led off, climbing round the rib after the others. When there was only fifteen feet of slack rope left, Dave shouted to Charlie, getting no reply. He shouted again that there was only eight feet left. Still no response. The rope pulled taut, but Dave heard no shout from Charlie. Acoustics were playing tricks on them, for although Dave and Charlie were only 130 feet apart they could not hear each other. Yet Pete Farrell, several hundred feet further along the ridge, could hear both of them clearly and, realizing what was happening, acted as liaison between them. Charlie would shout a message to Pete Farrell, and Pete would shout it back to Dave. Dave's replies to Charlie would follow the reverse route. I could hear the shouting from the ice-cave and wondered what was happening. Pete Farrell passed on the message to Dave that he was to start climbing. The mist, which had descended soon after dawn, suddenly cleared for a few minutes, and Dave could clearly see Pete Farrell halfway up the rock-gendarme on the other side of an open amphitheatre formed by the curve of the ridge.

Dave crossed the rib to join Charlie; then together they crossed the second rib onto the snow saddle. The sun was making a brave effort to break through the cloud, and the glare off the snow was enough to upset Charlie's sense of balance momentarily. He was climbing without snow-goggles, having given his to Dave, who had broken his own earlier that morning.

As he crossed the saddle, Dave could see Pete Bebbington and Graham ahead, already on their way up the gendarme. A steep snow-ramp led from right to left a third of the way up the gendarme, and it was on the top of this that Graham was belayed. Pete was half way across a fifteen-foot traverse that led into the snow and rock gully. He was climbing towards the rope down which they had abseiled the previous day from the top of the gendarme. Then clouds swirled down to blot them out completely from the view of Charlie and Dave, who were anyway engrossed in their own climbing. By the time these two reached the bottom of the snow-ramp, the gendarme was completely clear. They assumed that Pete and Graham were already over the top and were climbing down the other side.

The fixed rope hung away from the ramp, touching the snow-field about fifteen feet below the point where Charlie and Dave had stopped. They had just decided to climb down the fifteen feet and clip onto the rope, when they noticed an ice-axe lying in the snow. It appeared at first sight to have been tied to the end of the rope; but when Charlie climbed down to investigate, he discovered that it had nothing at all to do with it. Charlie assumed that Graham must have dropped it while climbing the gendarme. Graham, who habitually carried a spare ice-axe, would not have been unduly worried about the loss of this one—especially if he had seen it land in a prominent position and had assumed that Charlie or Dave would pick it up as they climbed past. There were no signs of a fall, nor had any cries been heard. They had no reason to suspect an accident. Putting the ice-axe in his pack, Charlie clipped onto the rope and continued up the ramp.

Ten feet or so up the ramp the soft snow changed to firm and compact snow, with hard ice at the top. The two previous ropes appeared to have belayed at this point, or slightly below it. Charlie did not trust the hard ice at the top of the ramp, so Dave found a secure belay in the snow at its foot. Charlie, already clipped onto the rope, thought he had enough rope to reach the top of the gendarme in one pitch and therefore started climbing. He was pulled up short ten feet below the top, but on a good stance with a secure belay. Dave clipped onto the fixed rope and started climbing up to Charlie. The ramp was straightforward climbing. At the top there was an awkward move off the hard ice and onto the traverse. The traverse itself, over loose rock that had few holds, was covered with a deceptive covering of snow and was very unpleasant.

Dave had clipped onto the end of the fixed rope and had not bothered to coil it as he climbed. The slack consequently formed an ever-increasing loop trailing behind him. As he reached the end of the traverse and began to climb up the gully, the rope snagged. He was unable to free it from where he was, and, to the accompaniment of continuous cursing from Charlie, he climbed back down to the traverse and freed the rope. This operation cost them half an hour. Dave coiled the rope round his shoulders and climbed up to Charlie.

Further on along the ridge just below the north summit, Pete Farrell and Vic watched them climb onto the top of the gendarme. Pete Farrell was uneasy. He thought that by this time he should have seen Pete Bebbington and Graham, but they were still nowhere in sight. He shouted across to Dave Condict and asked if he could see them. Dave shouted back that he couldn't and that the last time they had seen them was on the gendarme. From where Pete Farrell stood with Vic he could see down onto the glacier, 3,000 feet below. On it he could make out a dark spot that he could not remember having seen on the way up the previous day. Assuming that it was a rock that had fallen off the face, he dismissed it from his mind. Vic and he climbed over the ridge and abseiled down over the north summit on their way back to the ice-cave.

After their exchange of shouts with Pete and Vic, Charlie and Dave clipped a karabiner into a piton at the top of the gendarme. They abseiled from this down onto the ridge, to avoid the difficult rock-pitch that they had climbed the day before. The ridge had now become even more unstable as a result of the successive crossings of the party; and slow, careful, deliberate climbing was required along the delicate route. As they approached the north summit they were hailed again by Pete Farrell who had now reached the ice-cave. He was standing with Vic on the veranda, shouting to ask had they seen Pete Bebbington and Graham. The reply was the same as earlier: 'Not since the gendarme.' Pete Farrell and Vic disappeared back into the ice-cave, and Dave and Charlie continued climbing.

By then, they were climbing very slowly, partly because Dave was tired, and partly because every step had to be tested. The cornice below the north summit had become very precarious, with every other step collapsing. At one point Charlie leant heavily on his axe and pushed a hole right through the rotten ice. Bending down he could see Dave Condict through the hole below him, his head bowed and looking half-asleep. Charlie hoped that Dave was more alert than he appeared to be, and that he was prepared for any emergency. They reached the two-piton belay at the top of the ice-wall, threaded the rope through, and abseiled down. The abseil took them over the overhang; and as they descended they showered splintered ice and broken niches onto the now barely discernible traversing line which ran beneath the overhang.

By the time they reached the traverse the sun had gone down behind the ridges and the air had become very cold. The cloud had thickened, and they landed at the bottom of the abseil in the gloom of approaching night. Both were very tired. Attempts to pull the abseil rope down from the pitons failed, as it had snagged. In their tiredness they blamed each other, swearing furiously. They had fortunately taken up the fixed rope off the gendarme; this Dave now sorted out and coiled into a double length. They tied onto this rope and set off along the traverse. Silently they climbed quickly under the overhang, up the snow-gully and onto the ridge. They calculated that another two rope-lengths would bring them back to the ice-cave, and, feeling happier, began to talk again. A full run-out on the rope took them to the short ice-wall directly above the cave. Here they slipped their rope over a piece of Dexion that they found hammered into the hard snow, and abseiled down to the traverse leading onto the veranda. A few tired steps brought them onto the veranda and into the ice-cave.

There they found me, alone. Pete Farrell and Vic had passed through two and a half hours before and had climbed down the face to the ice-basin camp, so as to make more room for us in the cave. Pete Bebbington and Graham had not arrived.

Earlier, while I was reading *War and Peace*, I had heard Pete Farrell's voice somewhere on the ridge. Though I could hear quite clearly what he said, I failed to hear anyone reply to him. I went out onto the veranda and was surprised to find that the clouds had lifted. I could see along the ridge as far as the south summit, yet although I could still hear Pete Farrell's voice I could not see him. I was able to take some photographs before the clouds came down again, bringing the cold air with them. Pete had stopped shouting, and I went back into the cave.

I was startled when Pete Farrell suddenly appeared on the veranda at two-thirty. I had not expected any of the party back until the following morning. He told me of the successful ascent while he took in the rope from Vic, who soon joined him on the veranda. With the gas stove that they had brought back I was able to brew up a drink for them while they rested and told me about the ridge. Pete Farrell was uneasy. Every few minutes he would climb out onto the veranda and shout 'Pete' and 'Graham'. There was no reply.

They told me that they had decided to climb on down the face to the ice-basin camp that afternoon, to make more room in the cave. After the drink they prepared to leave; but before they left Pete Farrell went once again onto the veranda. He could see Dave Condict on one of the snow 'bumps' approaching the north summit. He shouted to ask Dave if he had seen Pete or Graham, to which Dave replied that he hadn't. I asked Pete how far behind the others were. He told me that I could expect Pete and Graham back within the hour, while Charlie and Dave Condict were still two and a half hours away. Then Pete Farrell abseiled down the gully out of the cave, followed soon after by Vic.

An hour after they had climbed out of the cave I began to brew a drink for Pete and Graham, though there were still no signs of them. Pete Farrell had passed on his uneasiness to me, and I too began to climb out onto the veranda shouting to Pete and Graham. And I too received no reply.

It said something for Pete Farrell's judgement that two and a half hours later to the minute, I heard voices outside. Climbing

34. The gendarme on the ridge between the north and south
summits

35. The south summit of Rondoy

onto the veranda, I saw Charlie traversing across to the cave, and asked him where Pete and Graham were. He replied by asking with surprise: 'Aren't they already here?' He told me what he knew while Dave was climbing down: of how the last time that they had seen Pete and Graham was on the rock-gendarme, and of the finding of the ice-axe.

Soon Dave too was in the cave and they were both eating the soup-stew that I had prepared from such remnants of food as I could find. I plied them with questions as they ate. Could the ice-axe simply have been dropped, or did it look as though it had been thrust in by someone falling? No, they replied; the axe was lying on the snow with its pick pressed in quite lightly. Could they possibly have gone off route and be bivouacking for the night? Again they replied; no, it would have been impossible for them to stop anywhere without Charlie and Dave seeing them as they passed. Could they have abseiled directly over the ridge and, bypassing the cave, have climbed straight down to the basin? This would have been possible, though very unlikely, since Pete and Graham would have known that we should worry at their non-appearance.

One by one, all the possibilities were ruled out. We each knew that they could only have fallen off the ridge and now be lying at the bottom of one or other of the faces. But we could not admit it to each other.

It was dark soon after Charlie and Dave arrived, and it had begun to snow heavily. We put up the Zarsky to block one of the entrances and some of the holes in the ceiling. There was nothing we could do that night, and we sat talking late, Dave and I now smoking the last of his cigarettes. We put off all decisions until the morning. Even then we still hoped that we might be surprised by Pete and Graham suddenly climbing in off the veranda.

In the morning, although there were two inches of fresh snow in the cave, the clouds had disappeared and the sun was shining. We realized that whatever else we did, it was essential to stop

Pete Farrell and Vic from climbing down from the ice-basin to base camp. While we talked over possible plans, we watched the tents in the basin until we saw someone move. Then Charlie began catching the sun on the lid of a milk tin while I polished the biscuit-tin lid, which would give a much bigger flash. I took over from Charlie and, catching the sun on the lid, sent the beam backwards and forwards across the tents. While talking things over we relieved each other at this signalling, which we kept up for two hours.

It was obvious that neither the weather conditions, nor the strength of the three of us in the cave, would enable us to send a rescue party out along the ridge, in case Pete and Graham had fallen onto a ledge and were waiting for help. Dave Condict and Charlie were completely exhausted, and I was not experienced enough to climb with any speed along a difficult route of which I knew nothing. The question was whether all of us ought to stay in the cave, all of us to climb down, or two only of us climb down to tell Vic and Pete Farrell the news.

By ten-thirty we had decided that Charlie and I would climb down the face. Charlie was against starting in the bright, hot sunlight, arguing that the fresh snow that had fallen during the last two days would be melting and soft, making the face dangerous. He wanted to wait till it was dark and the snow frozen. I argued back that we had, morally, no choice; and that, provided we made sure that neither moved without adequate protection from the other, we should be pretty safe.

There were three reasons for leaving someone behind in the cave: (a) Dave felt that one should be there in case Pete and Graham turned up after all; (b) two could move much faster down the face than three could; and (c)—which was more complicated—that although we couldn't be sure that Vic and Pete had seen our flashing signal, we knew they wouldn't leave the basin before mid-day. If, therefore, before then, we could get a rope of two out onto the face, they would realize that something must be wrong. For if they saw a rope of *three* on the face, they would merely assume that two out of the five were staying to rest in the ice-cave for another night. Furthermore, as Pete and Graham were the stronger pair, they would take for granted that these two—safely arrived at the ice-cave—were climbing down with me, while Dave and Charlie stayed behind.

Charlie and I left the cave at eleven o'clock, making good speed down the fixed ropes on the gully, traverse, and rock gully. I led off from the rock-ledge at the bottom of the rock gully and out onto the fresh snow on the face. Every step was filled with slushy snow, which collapsed as I put my foot in it. I moved very slowly and carefully across and onto the rock stance that we had all used on the way up. I pushed in my axe as a belay and called Charlie on. He refused to climb, saying that I should take the full 150-foot run-out, the stance I had taken being only forty feet from the gully. I shouted back that it would be too risky, given the condition of the snow, to take the full run-out onto the first of the ribs, where we both knew there was no sound belay. Charlie still refused to climb. Our nerves were already strained and we began to curse at each other. While we were arguing we heard shouts coming from the basin. Looking down we could see that Vic and Pete Farrell had seen us and were shouting up.

The acoustics of the face were so good that, although they were more than 2,000 feet away, we could make out quite distinctly what they said. They told us that they had seen the flashing, and asked us what was wrong. Charlie shouted down that Pete and Graham were missing. Pete Farrell shouted back that they would climb up that night and that we were to climb down to the basin.

Charlie climbed across to me, leading through and over the snow-rib into the first of the snow-gullies. He hammered in a piece of Dexion, and when I had joined him we abseiled down the gully. The sun was now so hot that every move cost us a great deal of effort and we climbed very slowly. We led through all the way down, climbing in 300-foot pitches. When we reached the zig-zag above the overhang in the middle of the face, I met with another problem. Hitherto we had, for the most part, been climbing directly into the sun, our eyes adjusting to the intense light. On the zig-zags, however, as I reversed direction every twenty feet, the sudden change of light caused optical illusions and I had to climb even slower, more by feel than by sight. I told Charlie what was happening and he kept me on a tight rope, for which I was very grateful. It must have been nerve-wracking for him to watch me feeling my way down, but he was very patient. The lower half of the zig-zag path had been obliterated by the fresh snow, and we were forced to front-crampon down the last 100 feet to the stance in the overhang.

We had no time to rest, if we were to reach the basin before nightfall; so we stopped only to hammer a piton into the hard ice before abseiling down the next section. Charlie went first, and when I reached him he had already hammered in another piece of Dexion. While I rested, he abseiled the next 150 feet, which led him into the gully immediately above the main bergschrund. I followed as soon as I heard him shout that the rope was clear. As I descended, the sun disappeared and it became very cold. As soon as I had unclipped from the rope, Charlie began to pull it through. It snagged. Both of us pulled on it for all we were worth, but it still refused to budge. Cursing and swearing we gave it one almighty tug and it sprang off the Dexion like an angry snake. We tied on again and climbed together down the gully. The snow was worse than ever, the new snow having collected in the easier-angled gully. Both of us slithered down a few feet from time to time, being stopped by friction and our ice-axes.

In an attempt to reach the tents before dark we speeded up, and when Charlie climbed down the rock-pitch around the bergschrund at the bottom of the gully, he went on down to the platform. I climbed down the rock and moved after Charlie, following the rope, instead of looking for Charlie's footsteps. I found myself on a steep slope of soft snow. My feet suddenly gave way and I started to slide. Charlie watched from below, unable to help. I fell on my ice-axe, but the top layer of snow was too deep and too soft for it to grip. I spread out my arms and managed to stop myself by friction on the upper lip of a shallow crevasse. After that I moved much more carefully.

We almost ran across the platform and down the snow-ramp above the tents. At the bottom of the ramp, Charlie untied and left me to coil the rope while he went on to the tents to tell Pete Farrell and Vic what news we had. I coiled the rope, retrieved my goggles from the avalanche debris where they had dropped from the ramp, and slogged the last small slopes back into the camp.

When I arrived Charlie had passed on his news, and Pete Farrell was talking. He told us how he and Vic had had to climb down the last sections of the face in the dark the night before and had arrived at the tents tired out. When they had emerged from the tent that morning, to eat their breakfasts in the sun, they had seen the flashing coming from the ice-cave. They knew that it could only be a distress signal. They decided that it would be unwise to return at once up the face; for they were still tired, and would be in no physical condition to help anyone after climbing the steep face in the hot sunlight. They therefore planned to wait before acknowledging the signal, which they proposed to do by arranging the camp equipment to spell 'TONIGHT' against the snow. Then they would climb back to the ice-cave at midnight.

It began to snow heavily and we moved into the tents. Vic prepared a meal and filled a vacuum flask with black, unsweetened coffee for Charlie and me to drink for breakfast. They would have to take the stove up to the cave with them as the gas cylinder there was nearly empty. Charlie and I had left our sleeping-bags and my airbed in the ice-cave, to save whoever went back—even if only to fetch Dave Condict down—the effort of carrying their own. While Vic and Pete slept for the four hours before midnight and we waited to take over their sleeping-bags and airbeds, Charlie and I drowsed, half talking, half sleeping.

9

The End

At midnight we were roused by the alarm in Vic and Pete Farrell's tent. It had stopped snowing and it was a clear night; the moon had risen, which would aid their climbing. They made a quick breakfast, passed on their sleeping-bags to Charlie and me, and within twenty minutes of waking were on their way back up the face.

We were awakened again at ten o'clock, this time by the stifling atmosphere of the tent. The sun was well up, shining directly into the basin, whose curved walls focused its rays onto the camp plat-form. When we emerged from the tent the heat hit us. We both began to feel weak and dizzy, and every movement called for a few minutes' rest. Breakfast consisted of strong black coffee, sweetened with marmalade, and such biscuits and sweets as we could find. We looked up to the ice-cave to see if there was any movement. There wasn't, but further along, on the traverse line under the north summit, we could see somebody beginning to climb the rib that led to the summit ridge. We were surprised that Pete and Vic had reached so far in such a short time, and wondered what condition the snow and ice would be in, in the strong sunlight.

We began to break camp, leaving one tent up for the others when they came down. Charlie found some solid fuel which he put into a biscuit-tin, and melted down some ice and honey to make a warm, sweet and nourishing drink. It was twelve-thirty before we were ready to begin our climb down to base camp. The packs we carried were enormous, the largest we had been burdened with so far on the expedition. They must have weighed over 70 lb. We helped each other on with the packs and began our traverse across the basin to the exit point. It was slow, hard going. The basin was filled with soft new snow, dragging at our feet and balling up on our boots. Small avalanches had been falling all morning, some reaching to within fifty feet of the tents. We picked our way through the debris, having occasionally to take off our packs and pass them across to each other over the small crevasses. At one of the crevasses I had difficulty putting my pack back on, and Charlie gained 100 feet on me.

Charlie reached the next crevasse below the abseil rope two or three minutes before I did, and as I walked I watched him prepare to jump across. As he tensed to jump, the snow gave way under him and fell into the crevasse. He fell with his arms on one side and his feet on the other. He thrust his axe into the far side as he fell, and then balanced on it, pulling his feet across and standing up. When I reached the same point I cut away all the soft snow and ice before I jumped, making sure that I had a sound piece of ice both to take off from and to land on. The crevasse was S-shaped and had therefore to be crossed twice. At the second crossing-point Charlie decided to throw his rucksack across ahead of him. It was difficult to throw the awkward, heavy pack so far, and it fell into the crevasse, wedging itself about eight feet down, so that he was forced to climb down to recover it. Not having learnt from Charlie's misfortune, I tried the same technique— only, like him, to follow my sack down into the crevasse. Thus we expended twice the necessary effort on the crossing.

When we reached the rock and the fixed rope, Charlie decided that it would be easier to climb up first and haul the pack up behind him. He climbed up the rock quickly and I tied his rucksack onto the end of the rope. Half way up the sixty-foot rock pitch was a small overhang. While I sat at the bottom smoking and watching, but completely unable to help, Charlie sweated, swore, and strained for an hour and a half before he succeeded in hauling the pack over the overhang. He rested for a while and then threw the rope down to me. I decided to climb with my pack on, while

Charlie kept me on a tight top rope. At the overhang I balanced for a few minutes on two hand-jams. I thought that I was going to have to climb down again but, remembering the difficulty of sack-hauling, I strained for all I was worth, mantelshelved over the overhang, and arrived on the ledge beside Charlie. We sat for a while recovering our breath. I could see clouds beginning to blow up the valley, and wanted to carry on down to base camp before they or the darkness overtook us. Charlie, still feeling exhausted, rested a little longer while I set off along the rope traverse. To save myself having to climb down and back, up the twin gullies, I followed the traverse line to a higher point and crossed horizontally to the foot of the fixed rope that led onto the ridge.

The eighty-foot rock-wall was easy rock climbing, but it was difficult to balance with a pack that had begun to feel as though it was loaded with several hundredweight of lead. I stopped for a rest half way up and, looking round, saw that Charlie was beginning to descend into the gully. I continued on round the ridge to the top of the rock-walls and began to climb down. Charlie was out of sight by now and finding his own route. In one of the small chimneys my feet slipped and I fell a few feet, landing on a scree slope. I had tried to hold on with my left arm, but only succeeded in wrenching my injured left shoulder again—the one I had damaged when I fell on the way up the ice-face. While I was sitting on the scree Charlie came into view. We had gone off route somewhere and found ourselves on difficult rock. The packs were forcing us to move carefully and slowly, which worried us, for the clouds had closed in and looked threatening.

It was some time before we reached the top of the grass gully. It was by then after four o'clock and the sun had disappeared. We didn't bother to stop and put on warm clothing. I set off down the gully which was full of loose rocks that whistled past me as Charlie started down behind. At least, most of them whistled *past* me! At a cry of 'Below!' from Charlie, I pressed myself against the gully wall, to be almost immediately knocked off balance by a rock hitting my pack. Deciding to get out of the gully as fast as possible, I moved onto a rib and moved down, scrambling from one bunch of grass to the next.

By the time I reached the bottom of the gully it had begun to snow. Charlie was tired and climbing slowly; so, as I could not help him, I carried on down towards base camp. When it started to snow more heavily I stopped to put on my anorak and shouted to Pete Westnidge in base camp that we were on our way. Eager for the comforts of the kitchen tent, I started to run down the last slopes—or rather, I just took my brakes off and let the slope carry me with it. The pack jogging up and down hurt my shoulder, but I reckoned that I would gladly suffer that in order to be back in camp more quickly.

When I jumped the last few feet across the river into base camp it was to find a huge plateful of steaming stew ready for me. Pete had seen the two of us several times during the day, and had thought that all seven of us were on our way down. I told him that Pete Bebbington and Graham were missing and that there was now no hope. I told him all I knew. He sat quietly, listening. As soon as I had finished talking, Charlie came into the camp. It was dark by then and the snow was heavier still.

We were sitting in the kitchen tent, talking and smoking, when suddenly the storm broke. It was the first time during the expedition that a storm had come right into the valley, and it seemed to be trying to make up for the delay. It was a storm to end all storms. It felt as though all the elements were having their last fling before giving up for ever. The heavy snow reduced visibility to a few feet, the strong wind turning each hard snow-flake into a bullet. The thunder roared round the valley, the lightning flood-lit the mountains. We hoped that the other three were not out in it; and Charlie and I were grateful that we had reached base camp before it broke.

In one of the lulls we went out and looked up at the face. Half way down we were surprised to see three lights. Pete Farrell, Vic and Dave Condict were still on the face in the middle of the storm. It must have been like hell itself up there. A flash of lightning blotted out the torches and, as blackness fell back into the void between us, we saw that one of the lights was appreciably lower. At that distance it could only mean that they were abseiling. We stood in the snow for a while watching them as they began abseiling down the last gully until clouds filled the basin and hid them from our sight. As the storm built up again we went back into the kitchen tent, hoping that the three on the face would be all right.

By the time the storm had calmed down and we had re-emerged from the warmth of the kitchen tent to settle for the night, the lights had disappeared from the face. I moved in with Pete Westnidge. As we lay in our warm sleeping-bags neither of us felt much like sleeping, and we talked and smoked late into the night. Pete told me how puzzled he had been by the movements on the face.

The morning after we had left base camp he had seen our rope of three, and Charlie and Dave starting the traverse below the ice-cave. He had watched us through the telescope until we had disappeared into the mist. When he saw the weather conditions the next morning he half expected that all seven would be coming back. Visibility never improved enough for him to see the six on the ridge. When nobody appeared on the face the following day (the day of the accident) he worked out that either six had gone to the summit, or else that we were all sitting in the ice-cave, waiting for the weather to improve. Later in the day he was puzzled to see a rope of two (Pete Farrell and Vic) appear over the ridge and begin to climb down the face. It was almost five o'clock when he saw them, and he wondered why they should be starting down the face so late that they would have to climb down in the dark. They were only visible to him for a quarter of an hour, as clouds filled the basin and blocked his view; and he was unable to see if any more ropes began the descent.

The End

When another rope of two—Charlie and I—appeared on the face at eleven the next morning, he began to wonder what was happening and hoped somebody would soon be down to let him know. He did not see Vic and Pete Farrell climb back up to the cave during the night, so that when a rope of three emerged from the cave late the following afternoon, he assumed that everyone was on their way down.

He was entertained that afternoon by an Indian who set fire to the grass slopes opposite the camp, to kill off the old and hard grass. At one time an area 300 yards by fifty yards was ablaze, burning into the night, and giving off so much light that he could almost read by it inside his tent. Although the wind blew the flames away from the camp site, he was grateful that the stream was between.

Meanwhile Pete Farrell and Vic, after leaving Charlie and me in the ice-basin camp, had made remarkably good time up the face. They reached the ice-cave at five o'clock, just four hours forty-five minutes after setting off. Dave Condict was startled when they climbed into the cave: he hadn't expected anyone to arrive in the middle of the night. At six, after they had breakfasted together, Pete and Vic left Dave alone in the cave again and climbed back up to the ridge. They went back along this, past the north summit, and reached the rock-gendarme where Pete Bebbington and Graham had last been seen.

From there they searched the head of the snow-gully that led from the bottom of the gendarme onto the 3,000-foot face. There were no signs of the missing climbers. There were not even any marks in the snow that could have suggested a fall. The only possibility was that either Pete or Graham had fallen off the gendarme, pulling the other with him. They must have fallen clear of the gully and over the overhang. Below the overhang was a drop of over 3,000 feet, onto the glacier. There could be absolutely no hope for their survival.

Pete Farrell and Vic searched what they could see of the glacier below, using the viewfinder of a telephoto camera lens, but could make out nothing. They returned along the ridge, picking up a fixed rope and a piece of Dexion as they went. The hot sun had melted the surface layer of ice, making it slippery, and everywhere there was a covering of soft, fresh snow. It was difficult work climbing back to the cave, calling for much skill and care; and it was the middle of the afternoon by the time they reached it. Dave Condict cooked a meal from what was left of the food, while Pete and Vic rested. After they had eaten they stowed everything into their packs, and all three set off down the face in the approaching dusk.

As Vic abseiled down the gully, the rope pulled a loose rock down on him, hitting his hip. It hurt and badly bruised him. Then, almost as soon as they had climbed out onto the face, the storm blew up. Climbing three on the rope was slow, so they decided to abseil down as much as possible. Wherever they could, they used the Dexion that Charlie and I had left, on top of which they had to hammer in all spare lengths that they carried. Even so it was a slow process, and it was not long before they had to switch on their head-torches. If a rope snagged at all it had to be left behind: there was no time to climb up and free it. Pete Farrell's North-Waller had to be left behind as an abseil point when they had run out of Dexion; and Dave Condict's ice-axe was used (and left) to give greater protection on a 300-foot abseil that took them over the bergschrund. They used the single line of the 300-foot nylon ropes to abseil on, tying one end to the Dexion. It took a lot of effort to cope with the rope's elasticity for, at the end of 300 feet, the give was more than ten feet.

They were completely exhausted when, at ten-thirty, they reached the half-buried tent in the basin. Pete and Vic had been climbing more or less continuously for twenty hours. They still had ahead of them the climb down to the base camp with heavy packs.

Their packs weighed more than 80 lb by the time they had

struck camp the following day. They had the same difficulty in getting out of the basin that Charlie and I had had the day before, losing over an hour on the sixty-foot rock-pitch. They climbed slowly across and down the rock. By the time they reached the grass gully it was dark, and they again had to climb by the light of their head-torches. At the bottom of the grass gully, Pete Farrell found a reserve store of energy and came down the last slopes to base camp at a tremendous pace, arriving in the camp over half an hour before Vic and Dave.

The three of us in base camp had been watching their progress since we first saw them begin the traverse out of the basin and across the rock-face. At first we watched them through the telescope, but later could only follow their progress while they were facing directly towards base camp, when their lamps were visible. When Pete strode into camp we had a hot drink and meal waiting for him. He told us as he ate how he and Vic had climbed back along the ridge as far as the gendarme, but had been unable to find any signs of Pete Bebbington and Graham.

When Vic and Dave arrived we sat in the kitchen tent discussing plans. There was no doubt that the next day would have to be a rest day. Pete Farrell and Vic had been climbing for six days, with very little rest. In that time they had virtually climbed Rondoy twice: a magnificent effort on their part, and a remarkable feat of skill and endurance. It was decided that, after a day's rest, Pete Farrell and Vic on one rope, Charlie and Dave Condict on another, should all climb up to the Oggione glacier to see if they could find the bodies.

I was to go down the following day to the farmer's house to cancel the *burros* we had ordered to take us round to the other side of the range. Later, when I heard from Pete and Vic what they had found on the glacier, I was to go down to Lima to inform the police and the British Embassy of the accident. It was essential that no news should be released until the next of kin had been informed. The only married member of the expedition was Pete

Bebbington, whose wife Betty—living alone in a one-roomed flat in London—was six months pregnant. Our hope was that the news could be kept quiet until one of Pete's family could break it and be with her during the first shock.

Exhausted, we all slept late the following morning. After lunch I went down to see the farmer. I told him that Rondoy had been climbed, and said that everyone was well. Several of his friends from down the valley had called, and I kept them supplied with cigarettes while we sat talking. They were full of praise for the ascent, and one of them told me that he thought Rondoy was the hardest mountain in the Huayhuash to climb.

I told the farmer that we should not after all be wanting the mules we had asked for, making the excuse that we had decided to attempt the climb of Jirishanca from this side. While we were talking, another farmer came in with two horses. I asked him if he would hire me one to ride to Chiquian, saying that I had to go down to the hospital in Lima. He answered that he had to go to Chiquian himself, and readily agreed to hire me one. So I arranged for him to come to the camp three days later, when we would ride down to Chiquian together.

When I arrived back, nobody was to be seen except Vic, who was walking round the quiet camp site making up packs of food for four days' climbing—the time they expected to spend looking for the bodies. When I told him that I had managed to hire a horse, Vic replied that, while I was out, the plans had been changed, and that he himself would now be going down to Lima. It was obviously better that someone who had been along the ridge and perhaps seen the bodies should go down to inform the authorities. Vic said that he would walk down, so I decided to take advantage of the horse I had booked to go down to Lima anyway, at my own expense, to have my shoulder (which had seized up) seen to.

At eleven the next morning Pete Farrell and Vic left the camp, followed after twenty minutes by Charlie and Dave Condict.

The End

Pete Westnidge and I watched them as they climbed up the river valley at the side of the moraine and up the grass gully. When they reached the scree slope that ran into the snowfield they traversed in the opposite direction to the route into the basin. After they had disappeared from view, Pete Westnidge and I whiled away the time playing dice. I lost more cigarettes.

In the afternoon the farmer paid a social call. We told him that the other six were up on the glacier, looking for a route onto Jirishanca. He stayed talking with us for most of the afternoon, and soon after he had gone we saw Pete Farrell and Vic coming across the snow-slopes at the top of the scree. We hadn't expected them back for three days. Just before dark, we saw them start the climb down the scree below the bivouac site. A little later we saw four lamps light up near the top of the last slopes above base camp.

We cooked up a stew, which was ready for them when they arrived. While they ate, they told us what they had found. Pete Farrell and Vic had reached the glacier first, and had just begun to climb down the difficult rock-pitch onto the glacier, when Charlie and Dave arrived. After a short traverse across the upper slopes of the glacier, they discovered that the dark spot that they had seen from the ridge was in fact Pete Bebbington's body. They shouted to Charlie and Dave, who were waiting at the top of the rock-pitch, telling them to stay where they were, as they would need help to get off the glacier.

As had been calculated, Pete and Graham had fallen off the gendarme, over the overhang, and down the face, to land 3,000 feet below on the glacier. It must have been instantaneous death. Graham had fallen into a crevasse. Pete was about forty feet above this crevasse, a little way up a steep ice-ramp in the extreme right hand (as faced) corner of the basin. They were still roped together.

Later, as Vic climbed back up the rock-pitch out of the basin, a falling rock hit him, cutting his face badly, close to his left eye. As soon as everyone was ready they set off back to base camp as fast as they could, in an attempt to arrive back before nightfall.

Rondoy

Dave Condict, even more than the others, had been shattered by the day's experiences, and did not feel that he could make a useful contribution to our discussion. After he had gone to bed, the rest of us sat up discussing the best policy for Vic to follow when he got back to Lima. We thought that the wisest thing would be for him to go straight to the Embassy, tell them the news, and ask them to keep it quiet until a cable had been sent to Pete's family asking them to break the news to Betty. We were all agreed that she must not hear it from the radio or newspapers. When we had laid out the general plan we went back to our tents for the night, leaving the details to be decided in the morning.

There was still an unknown factor. Derek Fabian was somewhere in the area looking for us. We were expecting him to arrive at any time. He had been a close friend of both Pete and Graham, and we wondered how he would feel, after crossing the world to climb with them, on finding that they had been killed. Nobody wanted to go on climbing: the expedition was over.

At five o'clock Derek Fabian walked into the camp, unseen by anyone. He was very badly shocked by the news; and seeing the effect that it had on him brought home to us the full realization of what had happened. We had gradually accepted the fact that Pete and Graham were dead. From the time we first knew they were missing, through the realization that there was no more hope, up to the finding and burial of their bodies, we had learned to live with the idea of their death. Now, the delayed shock hit us. Derek, stunned by the news, sat down on the path near the tents. When he had recovered and we were drinking tea, we welcomed his fresh advice on what to do. His first idea—decision, rather—was that someone must immediately return to London to tell their families exactly how Pete and Graham had died: he must also help Betty over the worst moments. Vic, who knew Betty best, was the obvious choice. What was left of the expedition's funds was not enough to pay his fare, but Derek offered to lend the money if the Embassy could not help.

The End

If Vic was to fly home, then Pete Farrell—the only other one of us who had been on the glacier and seen the bodies—would have to go with him to Lima and cope with the authorities. On his way through Chiquian he would arrange for the *burros* to move the expedition out. Vic and Pete Farrell decided to leave early in the morning and try to walk the thirty miles to Chiquian in one day. I was to carry with me on the horse enough food for the three of us during our stay in Lima.

The walkers left the camp at seven the next morning just as the farmer arrived—riding one horse and leading another for me. This was a sorry specimen, which looked as if it would have difficulty in carrying me the thirty miles. I had never ridden a horse before, except bareback for a few hundred yards on the trek in; so as I mounted, I prepared for an uncomfortable journey.

A few minutes after leaving the camp I had to stop, as the ruck-sack I was carrying was causing me a lot of pain on my left shoulder. It took half an hour to tie the pack satisfactorily onto the back of the saddle. At first I tried to guide the horse along the path the farmer had taken, but discovering that it knew the route better than I did, I let it have its head and sat back in the saddle, smoking.

We took a path that followed the bank of the lake for a while before climbing up onto the plateau. When we reached the crest of the first hill I reined in the horse. I turned round and for the last time looked up the valley to base camp; and beyond it, up to the ridge-line along from Jirishanca Chico, up and over Jiri-shanca, coming to rest on the peaks of Rondoy. I thought of the months we had spent in London planning the expedition to Rondoy, and how that expedition had been successful in its main intention—but at a price. I thought of Pete and Graham buried in the glacier; in death they had become part of Rondoy, the mountain that they had both loved and hated. With sadness welling up inside me I turned the horse's head round and kicked it into a trot to catch up with the farmer, who was waiting for me.

*Biographical Notes on
Members of the Expedition*

Glossary

Index

Biographical Notes on Members of the Expedition

PETER BEBBINGTON

The leader of the expedition. He had always enjoyed an outdoor life and was a keen Boy Scout in Wimslow, his home town, being awarded the Queen Scout's Badge before he joined the Navy for his National Service in 1956. His climbing only began when he joined the London School of Economics' Mountaineering Club in 1958. He quickly took to climbing, and his first long vacation was spent climbing notable routes in the Alps, including (for a day out) the Matterhorn. He went to Scotland at every opportunity to train in snow and ice conditions. After a short Alpine season in 1960 he went on with the L.S.E. club to a very full season in the Dolomites.

In 1961 came the opportunity that he had waited for: an expedition to the Peruvian Andes. Despite the tremendous amount of work he put into the organization of that expedition he still managed to graduate with honours in his geography finals in July. The 1961 expedition was a great success, conquering twenty-one previously unscaled peaks in the Cordillera Raura, as well as several notable second ascents. During that expedition Peter went on as an advance party into the Cordillera Huayhuash, but no climbing was possible as two members of the expedition had contracted frostbite on Sierra Santa Rosa. He had seen enough, however, to create a desire to return to the Huayhuash for an attempt on Rondoy, which Bonatti had failed to climb the previous year.

Peter was a tall, strong, tough, and independent man; a natural leader, whom friends and colleagues followed instinctively. He was always cheerful and ready with a word, or act, of encouragement. As a climber he was good on both rock and ice; and always ready to learn new techniques. After the 1961 expedition he stayed in Lima working for the English-language newspaper, the *Peruvian Times*. His articles for that paper aroused a great deal of local interest. His work took him throughout Peru, and in between trips he did much climbing in the Cordillera Central. He also found time to meet and eventually marry a member of the Lima English community.

DAVID CONDICT

Transport Officer. While at Dulwich College, Dave, a six-foot one-inch South Londoner, was an active member of the Scout group and, like Pete Bebbington, was awarded the Queen Scout's Badge. Also like Pete, Dave did not begin his climbing until he joined the L.S.E. Mountaineering Club, in his case not until 1960. Despite a low level of fitness, he rapidly increased his standard until by August 1962 he was well equipped for a successful Alpine/Dolomites season.

Suave and debonair in appearance, Dave could always surprise us with his ability to turn up in the most unlikely situations wearing a white shirt and tie. He is a careful climber and never takes risks; his cautious approach to every movement makes him slow, but at the same time a dependably safe, first-class climbing companion. He is an erudite conversationalist. He was always ready to undertake the less pleasant, thankless, tasks around the base camp.

PETER FARRELL

He began his climbing career from his native Manchester as a keen member of the Karabiner Club, but although he climbed extensively in the British hills and outcrops, he had had no Alpine experience by the time he emigrated to Australia at the age of eighteen. In Australia he worked as an electrician for a year before he moved on to New Zealand where he has settled. In addition to his work as an electrician he occasionally took jobs as a climbing guide and instructor. As a member of the Canterbury Mountaineering Club he seldom went climbing unless it was to tackle a major route. Although his training was minimal, his fantastic drive produced an amazing fitness—when walking he maintains a constant pace regardless of gradient or altitude.

Small and stocky in build, he was a born storyteller and would often sit, perched on a biscuit-tin, and keep us up until the early hours of the morning with humourous tales of life in New Zealand. He is a sober, dependable person, fond of children and of sleeping.

CHARLES POWELL

Food Officer. He is a Welshman by upbringing (a Londoner by birth), and before coming to the L.S.E. was a regular Captain in the Welsh Fusiliers (seconded to the West African Rifles). After leaving the Army, and before coming to the L.S.E., he spent a year hiking around Canada and the U.S.A. working wherever he could. He has been called the original rolling-stone.

As he led a very full student's life at college, climbing was only one of his many activities. When he left L.S.E. and went to the University of Wales at Aberystwyth he dropped his other pursuits, and from then on continually raised his climbing standards. After a spell of solo climbing at Chamonix in 1962 he joined the Mountaineering Association as an instructor in Austria. At the end of the alpine season he went to the North Wales branch of the M.A., but left in October to come to London and help in the organization of the expedition.

A little over six feet, Charlie is well built, heavy, and powerful. Like most Welshmen, he is, on the surface, hard and argumentative, but is sensitive underneath.

GRAHAM SADLER

Deputy Food Officer. A native of Birmingham, he too began his climbing with the L.S.E. club, and before the expedition had had four Alpine seasons, two Dolomite seasons, a great deal of winter climbing in Scotland, and extensive experience of rock climbing on almost every available rock-face in England and Wales. His was the serious attitude to climbing, and he seemed to accept each new climbing problem as a personal challenge. Continually training, he was probably the fittest member of the expedition. One of his idiosyncracies was always to carry two of everything—two sleeping-bags, two stoves, and two ice-axes—which was typical of his practical and tidy nature.

He was conscious of his height (five feet six inches) but, although small and slight, was wiry and strong. When climbing he was quick, steady, and safe.

DAVID WALL (*written by David Condict*)

Expedition Secretary and Treasurer. To the Peruvian hill-dwellers David was an awesome sight. Towering six feet three inches, ginger haired and bearded, lean-framed and bespectacled, he carried his air of brusque purposefulness and his soft, but strong and fastly spoken Northern accent, with such assurance that they came to regard him as a survivor of some lost, mythical, race of gods.

Most of us had become used to David's strong will, his enormous love for and knowledge of books, and his unintelligible accent, during three years of weekend rock climbing from L.S.E. A lengthy Alpine season with Pete Bebbington in 1962 left Pete in no doubt as to his ability on snow and ice. Accustomed since childhood to high hills he has become a seasoned climber—witness his election to the Climbers' Club.

His drive might leave the South Americans baffled, and the expedition members irritated, but it produced results. Most important of all was his role during the vital and chaotic months of March, April, and May of 1963. David took time off from his crowded research into inflation theory at the L.S.E., and turned his room—just ten minutes walk away from the college—into the expedition headquarters. From there he ran, telephoned and wrote his way around London. Amidst all this, he found time to become engaged.

VIC WALSH

Equipment Officer and Expedition Photographer. From his native London he joined the Air Force as a regular and was sent to the Scottish section of the Mountain Rescue. Later he had postings to the Middle East and East Africa where he was able to climb extensively. At twenty-three he left the Air Force and emigrated to New Zealand, settling in Canterbury. He joined the Canterbury Mountaineering Club where he met Pete Farrell, and together they pioneered a number of first-class routes in the New Zealand Alps—including the first ascent of the formidable east face of Mount Cook. The two of them formed the advance party of the 1962 New Zealand expedition to the Peruvian Andes (see the Alpine Journal of June 1964 for an account of that expedition), and it was during their stay in Lima that they met Pete Bebbington.

Vic is a first-class mountaineer, combining competence, determination and stamina to produce an impressive ability in all conceivable conditions. Generally quiet and easy going, he has a witty infectious humour which kept us laughing in the long evenings at base camp. Independent and practical, he would often go off on his own on a photographing excursion while the rest of us lay sun-bathing in base camp.

PETER WESTNIDGE

Deputy Equipment Officer. A native of Dronfield in Derbyshire, he was more or less brought up on the gritstone outcrops of the Froggatt and Stanage areas. By the time he arrived at L.S.E. in 1960 he was already an accomplished rock climber—although he had never actually set foot on a mountain. He was so keen that soon after being accepted for L.S.E. he hitch-hiked down one weekend to examine the climbing possibilities in the London area. He took to mountains rapidly and spent a great deal of his university career—vacation and term time—climbing throughout Britain. He had an impressive first season in the Chamonix Alps and also in the Dolomites in 1962, and was a natural choice for the expedition, although he hesitated for some months before before agreeing to join us.

His tough, stocky body looks out of place in a town, and he only appears natural and at ease half way up a rock-face thinking about the next move, a cigarette characteristically hanging from the corner of his mouth. At first meeting, he is shy and withdrawn, yet he has a deep sense of humour which was evident on the expedition—even after a broken ankle ended his share of climbing.

Glossary

ABSEIL   Abseiling is the process of lowering oneself down a rope fixed vertically over a steep or overhanging section of a climb. Used to overcome a difficult climbing problem or for quick descents when speed is essential.

BELAY   To belay is to fix oneself onto the rock or ice for safety when not actually climbing. A rope from the climber is fixed around a spike of rock or through a piton hammered into the rock or ice expressly for that purpose.

BERGSCHRUND   The gap or crevasse left round the upper rim of a glacier or snowfield, as the ice or snow moves downwards; it usually provides a difficult obstacle to any attempt to climb from the snowfield to the ridge of the mountain above it.

CAGOUL   A large anorak designed to fit over a Duvet.

CORNICE   A thin overhanging lip of snow-covered ice formed by the action of wind. They have a tendency to fall away, especially when stood on, and constitute a dangerous hazard. The particularly dangerous ones on the ridge connecting the north and south summits of Rondoy prevented Bonatti from reaching the higher summit.

CRAMPON   A framework of tempered metal with 10/12 short spikes, which is strapped onto a boot to facilitate movement on hard snow and on ice. The front two spikes project horizontally forward, and 'to front-crampon' is to climb on a steep face by means of kicking in these two spikes, and balancing on them and on the pressed-in pick of an ice-axe.

DEXION   Trade name for two- to three-foot lengths of L-shaped metal with numerous holes punched in it. All but three inches of it is hammered into the ice and a karabiner is clipped into it. A rope is threaded through the karabiner and used for abseiling. It has become an essential item of climbing equipment.

DUVET   A down-filled jacket used in low temperature conditions.

GENDARME   Also known as a sentinel. A rock obstacle rising up from and preventing progress along a ridge. It alludes to a policeman preventing traffic from moving along a road.

HAND-JAM   The bracing of a hand inside a crack which enables the climber to balance his body from it.

KARABINER   A small oval-shaped piece of metal with a part of one side forming a snap link gate, enabling rope to be clipped into the oval. On the principal of a safety pin, or the clip on a dog's lead.

LONG-JOHNS   Ankle-length woollen underpants.

MELT-WATER   Water flowing off a glacier, melted by the action of the sun during the day.

MANTELSHELF   Verb. To raise oneself onto a ledge of rock shaped like a mantelshelf, by means of downward pressure on the palms of the hands.

NORTH-WALLER   A shortened ice-axe with a hammer head used on steep ice-walls where pitons have to be hammered in.

PITON   A blunt dagger-like piece of metal having various shapes to suit the cracks into which they are driven for use as belays. Those intended for use on ice are longer and generally serrated.

PITON-HAMMER   A heavy-headed hammer with a short handle used for driving pitons into rock or ice.

RAMP   A formation of rock, snow, or ice giving easy access between two different levels.

ROPES, FIXED   A rope fixed across a difficult section of a climb and left in that position.

ROPES, TOP   A rope connecting a climber to someone above him, usually his leader.

SÉRACS   Pinnacles or pillars of ice of various shapes into which a glacier is sometimes broken when it reaches a steep slope.

SLING   A closed loop of rope.

TENSION STANCE   When—because it is impossible or unnecessary to provide a secure belay—the climber at a stance protects his companion by bracing himself against the rock or ice, this position is called a tension stance. Frequently used by French climbers instead of the normal belay.

TRAVERSE   A move made horizontally across a section of a climb.

ZARSKY SACK   Trade name for a tent-like shape of nylon hung from pitons on a face when a night out on the mountain is unavoidable.

Index

175

Index